Charles H. Hood

Walmart's EGONOMICS

The Greed Behind the Smiley Face

FOREWORD

I have found Chuck's story to be fascinating and one which all of America should read, especially those thinking of doing business with Wal-Mart.

I too have experienced the Wal-Mart way of doing business, but from a different perspective — representing clients. I, as an attorney, have represented clients who did business with Wal-Mart, and have had success in our lawsuits. The research I did in representing these clients, on each occasion, has convinced me that Sam Walton was the creator of Wal-Mart's ways, and nothing to my knowledge, has changed since his death. The story that Chuck tells in his personal experience with Wal-Mart seems to confirm my experiences. Experiences, again, that my clients had in dealing with Wal-Mart before Sam Walton died.

Certainly the greed factor that I experienced has grown, as Wal-Mart has grown. Unlike Wal-Mart's management of past decades, I am told that today's management owns huge homes and luxury automobiles as well as many have country club memberships ... that they live their lives in the lap of luxury. There's nothing wrong with any of this, in my opinion, but the question I always like to ask is, "How did they get their money for all of these toys?" Was it fairly gotten or was someone wrongfully taken advantage of in the process? I believe you will find the answer to this question as you read Chuck's book. Even with these cultural changes that I am told about, there seems to be one constant that remains, and that is — a rigidly held allegiance to the business mold and philosophy that Sam Walton put in place at the outset of Wal-Mart.

In my view, Sam Walton, was a master "Robin Hood," His operating philosophy has resulted in our seeing the doors closed to "mom and pop" businesses in small-town America, as Wal-Mart enters the town and drives prices down, I have been told, over and over again. What else would explain the closing of family businesses once Wal-Mart enters? I am also told that once the "mom and pop" businesses are closed that the Wal-Mart prices are raised.

The basic philosophy that I have seen and see in reading Chuck's book, is the method that Wal-Mart executives use in "hooking" non-suspecting vendors who, like Chuck, want to do business with Wal-Mart. All one has to know is how a fish is "hooked" and then reeled on to shore, for slaughter. As you read Chuck's book, look for the way that Chuck was "maneuvered," "manipulated," and finally "hooked." Make a game of it as you study the way it was done. See if you can see, through Chuck's experience, how he was "hooked." How he allowed Wal-Mart executives to "abuse" him in a way that he had never allowed before by one he was doing business with. Watch the masters at work.

The problem, as I have seen it through the years, is that Sam Walton has been "eulogized" so much since his death that he has taken on the image of being such a "wonderful guy," because of all his "giving." I would ask the question I asked earlier, "Where did the money come from that he 'gave' away?" Were there those that were wrongfully injured in the process of his gathering all of this money that he "gave away"?

Gary L. Richardson
Garyricharsonspeaks.com
Tulsa, Oklahoma

Gary Richardson is a trial lawyer and author of : *Black Robe Fever, Fear Is Never Our Friend, and Thank God They Ate the Apple.*

SPECIAL ACKNOWLEDGMENTS

This is a story that needed to be told. It is dedicated to the devoted men and women that comprised the management, service and support groups of AD-Dvantage Media Group, Inc. They believed, as did I, their tireless work in behalf of our company and Wal-Mart would be rewarded with long-term employment and the compensation and benefits associated with a job well done. Accordingly their jobs were extremely well done. Ours was a workforce that took immense pride, not just in what we were able to accomplish in our respective jobs, but in being a supplier to America's leading and largest retailer.

Further thanks are due to my long-time friend, fraternity brother and banker, Robert W. "Bob" Davis. Bob was chairman, president and CEO of Tulsa's F&M Bank. Although he is since deceased, Bob's insightful way of doing business, along with his willingness to "go out on a limb" if he believed in you and/or your project, was what enabled us – and others – to start a business, having only a patent as collateral.

Additional thanks go to my good friend and business partner Gary Young, whose honesty and integrity are examples for everyone; to my good friend, long-time business associate and creative guru, David L. Hicks, for his compelling cover design; to Joyce Gideon for her invaluable counseling, editing and public relations support; to Gary L. Richardson, famed Oklahoma trial attorney and author, for his invaluable counsel and further insight into the inner workings of Wal-Mart; to my New Yorker friend Gene Bay, who not only lived a part of my story, but has been a true friend for more than 35 years; and to the staff of Create Space for their support and patience in allowing me to postpone deadlines so many times, while I continued to change my mind relative to the presentation of my story. Finally, I owe an enormous thank you to my wife Judy, my ever-present editor, counselor, confidante, and the love of my life.

TABLE OF CONTENTS

PROLOGUE

The story you are about to read is a factual account of the attitudes, ego-driven actions and what we found to be the usual business practices that lie behind **Wal-Mart's constant outward facades of the feel-good smiley face and the powerful banner that touts their "everyday low prices."** It chronicles the nearly seven years of Wal-Mart's contract violations, unfulfilled promises and unexpected perpetrations experienced by ADDvantage Media Group, Inc. (AMG), a tiny, Tulsa, Oklahoma firm. AMG marketed the services of its Shopper's Calculators to the retail industry. The company was an in-store advertising company, driven by a calculator service (for consumers), with a space for product ad messages, and mounted on the handles of the retailer's shopping carts — in this case Wal-Mart's.

As the company CEO, I lived, witnessed, and knew our story all too well. But, before writing my story, I did a considerable amount of additional research. I hoped to determine just how unusual our experience had been, compared with that of others that had been — or had attempted to become — successful Wal-Mart vendors.

I also wanted to know if and how much Wal-Mart's business plan had changed since the death of Sam Walton. Were the warm and fuzzy eulogies attributed to him, after his death, accurate? Or had the legend of him being a "great guy" amongst "plain folks" simply been exaggerations that had become cover-ups for his founding of the same harsh, damaging principles and actions practiced by today's management?

The opinions of the people I spoke with varied, but most expressed confidence that today's management group is simply following the guidelines put forth by Sam Walton when he founded his soon-to-be retailing "goliath" — yet in a more mean-spirited manner.

Many of the people I spoke to had been run out of business, usually because Wal-Mart elected to circumvent them and go directly to the original source. And, when possible, Wal-Mart would actually become the manufacturer. But, either way Wal-Mart had been responsible for the closure of too many businesses — while Sam was alive and after his death — and their methodology was usually legal, despite being highly dishonorable.

One very strong opinion relative to Wal-Mart's greed and their accompanying business practices was given to me by Gary L. Richardson, a widely acclaimed attorney who in the past successfully sued Wal-Mart in behalf of his clients. His enormous amount of research, conducted in preparation for each trial, left him with the opinion that "nothing has changed. Wal-Mart does what Wal-Mart does — and has always done so, since day one."

Unfortunately, the repeated lies and devious actions of Wal-Mart's corporate management forced ADDvantage to close its doors and release its more than one hundred employees. This action was a necessity, and it was due solely to Wal-Mart's unfulfilled commitments in combination with its widespread egotism and unabashed arrogance.

This is a true story supported by more than eleven thousand pages of documentation, plus numerous tape recordings, nearly all of which substantiate Wal-Mart's misrepresentations and harmful actions that led to AMG's loss of millions of dollars. It is a detailed account of Wal-Mart's deceptive ways. We called it Wal-Mart's EGOnomics.

****

Although many towns, companies and people will tell you differently, the after-death legend of Sam Walton tells us that Sam Walton built his Wal-Mart dynasty by creating and building mutually beneficial partnerships with his employees, vendors and customers. These partnerships enjoyed high degrees of success because they were based on Sam's self-described "bedrock values of honesty, neighborliness and thrift."

Wal-Mart's employees were known as being the company's "associates," And They were supposedly treated accordingly. Furthermore, as Sam pointed out, his true partners were able to "put the needs of their egos behind the needs of the team."

The Sam Walton "Legend" further tells us that Sam's founding "plain folks" philosophies and values were unquestioned and rigidly adhered to until April 6, 1992. That was the day Sam Walton died. Unfortunately, following Sam's death, many of his previously loyal members of management chose to leave the team and its guiding bedrock values. In doing so, they re-positioned their egos to the forefront of their actions, making adjustments for no one. As a result, those store employees Sam previously identified and treated as being his company's "associates," are now even self-described as being treated much more like "serfs."

Lawsuits against Wal-Mart have numbered in the thousands annually. *Forbes* reported the '05 average as being "one filing each thirty minutes." The Equal Employment Opportunity Commission (EEOC) contends that it does everything possible to avoid filing lawsuits. Its policy is to never file a lawsuit against anyone, until it has exhausted all efforts to work out a voluntary agreement with the company deemed to be "in violation" of the law. But, despite this operating philosophy, the EEOC has filed multiple suits against Wal-Mart on behalf of Wal-Mart employees, in nearly every discrimination category, inclusive of age, race, gender, and nationality.

Their filings even included one that addressed the use of "wetback" terminology allegedly being used to address and describe Wal-Mart's Hispanic employees. The list continues, including multiple allegations of forcing employees to work overtime without additional pay, the underpayment of hourly workers, etc. Many of the lawsuits have dealt with wage and hour violations; and in nearly all cases, they address management's lack of respect for, and the lack of fair treatment of its lower-echelon, in-store employees.

Typifying Wal-Mart's frequent, devastating actions is the story of the manner in which they closed their store in Nowata, Oklahoma. It represents Wal-Mart's not-so-bedrock values —misrepresentation, dishonesty, betrayal and the ever-present lack of respect for its "partners."

In response to the rumors of their departure from the town of Nowata, and in advance of closing their Nowata outlet, Wal-Mart placed a sign in front of the store reading: ***"THE RUMORS ARE FALSE. WAL-MART WILL BE HERE ALWAYS."***

Shortly after posting this sign, the Nowata store was closed. When queried about the closing of the store after the posting of the sign, Wal-Mart officials contended that it was not a store "closing," but rather a "consolidation." This appeared to be a dramatic example of what many people believe to have been Sam's business philosophy from the outset: Run the local businesses out of business with "everyday low prices," then hike the prices." And, in the case of Nowata, Wal-Mart had done just that to the town's previous small business residents. Now they intended to steal the town's supportive tax base while moving their mega-marketing machine to a larger demographic. And in doing so, they were forcing the Nowata citizens to drive extra distances for nearly all of their shopping — especially if they still wanted to enjoy "everyday low prices."

Semantics were meaningless to a community that now faced very serious problems. In fact these problems were so severe that the Nowata city manager made a trip to Wal-Mart's corporate headquarters in Bentonville, Arkansas to see its then-president, David Glass. While there, he virtually begged for compassion and help. Thereafter, neither he nor his town received either the badly needed help, or any type of response to his request. It was in view of this lack of response that the Nowata children developed the school-yard chant: "Wal-Mart, Fall Apart."

Unfortunately, this same chant has become far too meaningful to too many of Wal-Mart's past "partners." Many — like the citizens of Nowata — expected far more from their "partnerships" with America's largest retailer. But, in too many cases, high expectations have been to no avail for too many vendors and employees, alike.

It has been said that "America worships at the altar of 'everyday low prices.'" By doing so, these same shoppers allow Wal-Mart to get away with the ravaging of American wages, benefits and jobs.

Business Week has described the "everyday low prices" slogan as being "the core value of a cult masquerading as a company." In keeping with their underlying philosophy, Wal-Mart is known to lobby furiously in Washington for free-trade-deals that guarantee their ability to obtain goods made by pennies-per-hour labor forces. Wal-Mart_also scours the globe's sweatshops for the "cheapest prices." Seldom does a "Made-in-America" product label make it on a Wal-Mart shelf. In too many cases, even if the vendor is based in America, the product is too often made elsewhere in order for the vendor/supplier to meet Wal-Mart's pricing demands.

As *ABC News* reported in 2011, "More than 90% of the goods sold at retail in the United States were manufactured and shipped from foreign lands." As America's largest retailer, Wal-Mart must bear a large part of the responsibility for this severe lack of retail opportunities for American-made goods. And, perhaps of even greater importance, it must assume a like amount of responsibility for the enormous number of American manufacturing job opportunities no longer available to America's work force. Yet it is these same suffering, out-of-work Americans that continue to feed this growing "goliath."

Claude Harris, Wal-Mart's first buyer, spent a great deal of time with Sam Walton, and knew him quite well. He has been quoted as describing Sam's belief that his employees must "be good to people and fair with them. Lip service won't make a real partnership."

But, the inclusion of these values in their business relationships have long-since vanished — at least they never surfaced during the course of our "business relationship." Our relationship was filled with far too much "lip service," in combination with a continuing stream of outright lies and unfulfilled commitments.

Many long-time Wal-Mart observers will tell you that Wal-Mart's business philosophies and actions have not changed one iota since Sam opened his very first Wal-Mart "five and dime." Some will also tell you that Sam was the master in selling "cheap" and inferior goods to the poor (and today the unemployed) for low prices — and all the while receiving high praise. They will further tell you that even after Sam's death, their way of doing business hasn't changed. It is simply more of the same.

However, the huge numbers of "eulogies" since his death do bring into question just how much of Wal-Mart's dangerous and deceptive business model was created more than fifty years ago and how much was created after Sam's death.

Either way, I likened our experience to that of a cat severely wounding a mouse, then "playing with it" until its wounds forced it to finally succumb. Unfortunately Wal-Mart played the role of the cat and ADDvantage was the mouse, and we were dead from the outset.

It was as a result of Wal-Mart's continuing stream of lies to AMG's customers, coupled with their too many unpredictable and harmful actions — all of which were contrary to the guidelines specified in our contractual "partnership" agreement — that on January 18, 1995, ADDvantage Media filed a forty-million-dollar lawsuit in the U.S. District Court for the Western District of Arkansas, alleging "breach of contracts and corporate sabotage."

At the outset of our relationship with Wal-Mart, our company, ADDvantage Media Group, Inc., was a publicly traded company with a stock market value in excess of eighteen million dollars.

The day that our lawsuit was filed against Wal-Mart, AMG had a market value of less than three hundred thousand dollars.

Wal-Mart's slogan was

"Watch Out for Falling Prices."

We had no idea they would intentionally make this statement apply to us.

THE PREMISE OF OUR PRODUCT — THE SHOPPER'S CALCULATOR

The Shopper's Calculator was designed to benefit the retailer, the retailer's vendors (product manufacturers) and the retailer's customers. It is a calculator with an advertising image area that mounts on the handle of each of the retailer's shopping carts.

First and foremost, each Shopper's Calculator provides a meaningful service to the retailer's customers. The convenience of this cart-mounted calculator allows shoppers to track the cost of their purchases, deducting coupon values, etc., as they shop — enabling them to stay within their spending limits and budgetary guidelines. The Shopper's Calculator also allows its users to compare product sizes and values (cost per ounce, per pound, etc.) of the variably priced, variably sized packages offered for sale. And, the calculator also allows the consumer to calculate food content (calories, cholesterol, fat, salt, etc.).

However, the real and hidden value of the Shopper's Calculator is that when the consumer uses it to track money spent, it silently contributes to increased sales for the retailer. The calculator eliminates the shopper's need to "round-up" (i.e., sixty-five, seventy-five and eighty-five-cent purchases previously rounded-off to one dollar each in the consumer's mind, now showed a "calculated total of two dollars and twenty-five cents — 25 percent less than the rounded-up total of three dollars). In doing so, the calculator restores what were the retailer's previously "lost sales," and now allows the consumer to make more purchases with the same amount of dollars.

Extensive research has shown that when a customer mentally "rounds-up" amounts of purchases, he/she exits the check-out line having spent between forty-three and forty-six of the fifty dollars he/she intended to spend upon entering the store. By allowing the customers to track purchases, it allows them to spend all of their available dollars, thereby providing a service to the retailer's customers while recapturing what were the retailer's previously lost sales.

The secondary physical feature of the Shopper's Calculator is its advertising image area. The presence of an advertiser's product message in this space is virtually a "guarantee" of increased product sales. It works for one very simple reason. The advertiser's message is positioned "front and center" at the fingertips of each shopper throughout the entire shopping experience –– up and down each aisle, all the way to check out.

Nearly two million dollars' worth of research has validated the ability of the calculator to increase advertised product sales as much as 48 percent. Further attesting to the power of this advertising medium is research, which documented that 73 percent of the shoppers were able to recall precisely what product was advertised on their shopping cart calculator, after exiting from the store.

We were confident that ours was definitely a product that offered Wal-Mart further and almost endless sales and economic opportunities.

Part I — 1991

Chapter 1

Welcome to Wal-Mart!

JUNE 12, 1991

On what was soon to become a very warm and humid day in Arkansas, I made my initial trip to Bentonville in hopes of soon becoming a Wal-Mart vendor/partner. In years past I had made numerous trips to Bentonville on behalf of my advertising agency clients. The purpose was always the same – to present their national ad campaigns and the accompanying media schedules that would soon be airing in support of selling the products that Wal-Mart carried to the market place on my clients' behalf.

However, this was my first visit as a product salesman, on a mission to sell Wal-Mart on accepting a product designed to increase their sales. Unfortunately, I had no way of knowing that I was about to embark upon a seven-year "journey to nowhere" — one which would eventually void seven years of my business life and career. It's perhaps best described as being a total exercise in futility.

Accompanying me that day was Bill Atherton, a Tulsa entrepreneur and company board member, who at one time had been one of Pizza Hut's largest single franchisees. Although I had not known Bill too long, he had impressed me as being a classic example of a "man's man." Furthermore he possessed a great deal of charisma and just happened to be an extremely talented and successful businessman.

It was during Bill's many years in the pizza business that he had forged a lasting relationship with Sam Walton. The two of them had assisted one another in property acquisitions. On numerous occasions property had been purchased as the future home to a Wal-Mart store and a neighboring Pizza Hut, and vice versa. Bill and Sam had also become hunting companions. It was through this activity that Bill had become acquainted with David Glass, Sam's successor and Wal-Mart's then-president and CEO.

Today we were scheduled to meet with Glass for the sole purpose of introducing him and Wal-Mart's executive marketing personnel to the benefits of installing our product, the Shopper's Calculator, on all of their shopping carts in all of their stores. Our presentation was geared to appeal to Wal-Mart's need and greed — more ways to make money. It guaranteed Wal-Mart that their share of the Shopper's Calculator advertising program revenues would be no less than a guaranteed minimum of $2,000 per store, per year. In return, Wal-Mart only needed to allow us to install our calculators on each of their shopping carts in all of their stores, and then endorse the program to each of their vendors whose products were carried on their store shelves.

And, the $2,000 was an absolute minimal level of new revenue for Wal-Mart. Past experience told us that if Wal-Mart truly did endorse the program, their vendors would literally "stand in line" to participate. As a result, Wal-Mart would have the opportunity to share in their vendors' national advertising dollars — a category never previously available to them. But our in-store advertising qualified them for access.

Our past use of the Nielsen Company, and many others, for our in-store research more than validated the power of our Shopper's Calculator concept. In fact, in the words of one of the Nielsen company executives, "We can not put this in writing, but the increases in sales of the products advertised on the Shopper's Calculators exceed those of any study we have ever conducted," as did the ad recall numbers gleaned from Nielsen's exit interviews. We also knew that the Shopper's Calculator program offered Wal-Mart's vendors an exceptional opportunity to increase their sales volumes -- and potentially profits too -- from the sale of their products in each of the Wal-Mart stores.

It was a foregone conclusion that Wal-Mart would never allow any vendor to increase its margins. Consequently, the only way to increase profits was by increasing volume. Based on the test data gathered in previous installations in grocery stores, the calculator program offered each vendor a significant opportunity to do so. The program was a WIN-WIN-WIN for Wal-Mart, Wal-Mart's customers and Wal-Mart's vendors.

When we entered the reception room of Wal-Mart's corporate headquarters that morning, it was a typically busy day at the famed "Wally World." Both established and potential Wal-Mart vendors were aligned twelve deep in two single-file lines approaching the dual receptionists positioned at the front desk. Already the mini-amphitheater seating areas positioned to the left and right of the receptionists' desks were two-thirds full of sales men and women – the majority of whom were hoping for or anticipating a "home run" sales call.

Attesting to the "home run" hopes of those present, was one very excited salesman who was standing against the wall next to the end seat where I was waiting. He was on the phone, speaking loudly and very emotionally — obviously to his home office — telling them of his pricing needs for a potentially huge order. The conversation went somewhat like this: "They want to order 200,000 sets of our low-end line of sheets, in all sizes, and a like number of pillow cases. They will pay 'X' dollars each. (Pause) I know, I know we can't make them for that, but we have got to find a way. This is a sale we can't afford to pass up. It will solidify our Wal-Mart relationship for now and in the future. This is an opportunity that we must find a way to pull off."

Further attesting to the frantic atmosphere of this busy morning was the abrupt and harried response of one of the receptionists to the salesman who had been in line behind me. It was 10:50 a.m., and he very politely and respectfully told her his name and that he was there for his eleven o'clock appointment with a specified Wal-Mart buyer/employee. She promptly told him, in a tone betraying her annoyance, to "please take a seat. I am still processing the 10:45 a.m. appointments."

We were more fortunate. The fact that we were there to see David Glass at 11:00 a.m. made us much more welcome — and it was readily apparent that we had not disrupted her scheduling, even in the least.

At fifteen minutes after eleven, we were ushered into the surprisingly small and simple office that housed the simplistically attired, stern-faced David Glass.

The austerity of the room made it immediately apparent that no decorator had ever darkened these doors. His bookcase served as solid testimony to this. Positioned behind his purely functional desk and chair were rows of books and documents encased in a framework of bowed two-by-twelve boards spaced and held in place by cinder blocks of the same size and color as those used to construct the Sam's corporate headquarters across the street. Our initial reaction was that this office had been furnished precisely in accordance with Sam's wishes and his over riding corporate philosophy — "economics and low prices."

Although this office encounter certainly reinforced their philosophical point, we were later asked "in which of his offices" our meeting was held. Apparently his "real office home" was quite comfortable and very expensively decorated and furnished.

Our meeting with Glass was cordial and brief. The majority of our time was spent discussing and listening to the successes and failures of past game-bird hunts. Very little time was allowed for us to make our presentation. Instead, Glass asked that we leave copies of our presentation for him to review and distribute to his marketing executives. He then told us that we should wait to hear from a fellow Wal-Mart executive.

Although we were disappointed in not being allowed more time to tell and sell him on the unique benefits that our Shopper's Calculators could bring to Wal-Mart, we agreed that our mission had been a success. As we left their corporate headquarters, I was even further encouraged by the conspicuous lack of any luxury automobiles in the executive parking areas. Instead, there was a rather obvious abundance of American-made economy cars, nearly all of which were painted in very conservative colors.

It never occurred to me that this seemingly steadfast corporate culture, so obviously based upon American-made products, in combination with Sam Walton's proclaimed cornerstone values of "honesty, neighborliness and thrift," would soon make an abrupt change.

Perhaps it was Sam's oft-stated "bedrock" values and philosophies that were so appealing to Gary Young — my business partner and our company's CFO — and to me.

The underlying reason for their appeal to us undoubtedly had to do with our respective upbringings.

Each of us was raised by frugal parents who experienced life during the Great Depression. Even before either of us reached the age of twelve we were actively engaged in the American work force. Gary worked at his dad's service station, doing grease jobs, oil changes and auto details. I worked multiple jobs, delivering morning newspapers, selling shoestrings and shoe polish door-to-door, cleaning kennels for the local veterinarian, and washing the storefront windows of merchants in downtown areas. They were full and difficult schedules for each of us, but in both cases they led to meaningful funding for our respective college educations. Gary received a degree in accounting from Kansas State University. I received a degree in advertising from the University of Missouri — where Sam and David Glass also attended. It was probably our mutual "work backgrounds" that led us to wholeheartedly believe that the presence of our product in the Wal-Mart stores would be a "Win, Win" for Wal-Mart and for us.

Unfortunately, our projections for what we hoped lay ahead could not have been further from the forthcoming reality. But on this day, we were genuinely pleased and excited about the potential for our Shopper's Calculators fitting right in with the Wal-Mart corporate culture and its business philosophies — and playing a major role in the Wal-Mart marketing equation for years to come.

Furthermore, Glass had promised to disperse our presentations to their corporate marketing personnel. We also just knew that in doing so, there had to be an implied endorsement, right? Unfortunately, we had no idea of what lay ahead for us, all brought about by the corporate arrogance and egomania that runs throughout the halls of America's largest, leading retailer.

Chapter 2
Let the Games Begin!

JULY 6, 1991

Two weeks after our visit with Glass, we received a call from Wal-Mart's Dave Lienemann, advertising and pricing manager for Wal-Mart's Supercenters and Hypermarts. He asked that we come to Bentonville to discuss our product and programs. At that meeting we were advised that Wal-Mart wished to test our product in all of its Supercenters and Hypermarts. We were instructed to present Wal-Mart with programs and options that would guarantee Wal-Mart a steady stream of revenue, while they tested the service and sales-stimulating capabilities of the Shopper's Calculators.

(Note: Initial Wal-Mart presentation on pages 30-37 of Appendix.)

JULY 24, 1991

We returned to Bentonville to meet again with Lienemann and review our presentations, which consisted of two options. Proposal A guaranteed Wal-Mart $500 per year, per store, and allowed us to sell the advertising for 90 percent of all of the installed units. This left 10 percent of the calculators free for Wal-Mart to promote its private label products. This allotment would also provide Wal-Mart with a first-hand opportunity to do comparative testing and discover for itself the impact that the calculators would have on their store sales.

Proposal B allocated all units to our sale of advertising and none to Wal-Mart. The revenue guarantee was $1,000 per year, per store. In both Proposals A and B,

ADDvantage Media would assume all program expense, which included the cost of the units, the twice-weekly servicing (keeping the units clean and always being certain that all units were in good operating condition), all ad sales and printing expenses, etc. In return we were to be given the opportunity to install our Shopper's Calculators in all present and future Wal-Mart Supercenters and Hypermarts.

To assist us with our selling process, the contract specified that Wal-Mart would provide us with all necessary marketing data — store traffic counts, product sales numbers, monthly product sales comparisons, etc. These statistics were vital to the selling process, and we asked for them repeatedly. With each request, we were promised they would be "forthcoming." We never did show up.

Although at the outset of our program the number of stores totaled just ten, Wal-Mart had selected these store formats as their store concepts for the future, and they projected and anticipated the opening of nearly one hundred per year in the future. Wal-Mart would not be selling the advertising, but they were contractually required to provide us with their all-important program endorsements, as well as their supportive research data to facilitate the selling process. Finally it appeared as though we and Wal-Mart were on the same page.

AUGUST 6, 1991

I received a call from Dave Lienemann that morning telling me that our contract for Proposal B had been approved and signed with just one slight change. This apparently "insignificant" change was that Wal-Mart was to be guaranteed $2,000 per year, per store, as opposed to the original presentation amount of $1,000. But, we were to begin unit installations on all carts, in all stores, immediately.

We had priced our original presentations in anticipation of Wal-Mart increasing the revenue terms, but had not anticipated their being **doubled**. However, we agreed to terms in view of the overriding opportunity of being the **only** in-store media program offered in Wal-Mart's stores for the future – the highly acclaimed Wal-Mart Supercenters and Hypermarts. After all, it was Wal-Mart's corporate objective to become "America's largest grocery retailer." And they intended to do so through these same stores in which we were to be the sole in-store media — per our contract — that was allowed to sell in-store advertising within the Wal-Mart Supercenters.

If you couldn't sell advertising — inside these Wal-Mart stores — to vendors who generated 25 to 30 percent of their total sales through Wal-Mart's outlets, **where or what could you sell**, right? It was going to be wonderful having the "only game in each Wal-Mart town."

Although this date launched wild dreams and visions of enormous success, it was also to become one of historical infamy for the management and stockholders of ADDvantage Media, the Shopper's Calculator Company.

SEPTEMBER 1991

Shortly thereafter we received our signed contract and immediately began to work on the program. We prepared a news release announcing the terms of our new agreement with Wal-Mart and an introductory letter — to be sent to all of their vendor/partners — announcing the program, its accompanying advertising rates and Wal-Mart's all-important endorsement thereof. We then delivered the proposed news release and ad sales letter to Wal-Mart; and shortly thereafter both were approved for immediate release, with negligible changes.

Just one day after our news release was published and broadcast, I received a phone call from the then-president of Tulsa's State Bank. It was a "new business call" telling me that his bank was owned by members of the Walton family and that it would be wise for us to consider banking with him – now that we had a contract with Wal-Mart. I politely responded by telling him that he was most welcome to come see me to discuss it. His curt response was, "I'm not 'gonna' do that. You come see me when you're ready to do business." I didn't hear from him again, but his approach to doing business was of a style that we were to experience many more times in the future.

In accordance with Wal-Mart's request that we begin installing our Shopper's Calculators on their shopping carts immediately, we contacted all of the store managers to apprise them of our installation schedule, and the actual installations were under way in less than a week.

Although we were promised ten stores initially, we were only able to install eight of those ten. Unfortunately, a large percentage of the carts in two of the stores had been vandalized to the point of near non-use. They had no handles. Although they were capable of holding one's purchases, they were incapable of holding a calculator.

We reported the problem to Lienemann and were promised that the situation would be rectified immediately — via either making the necessary repairs, or providing new carts. But, like so many other promises to come, none were ever fulfilled and although our contract "guaranteed" us the opportunity to sell advertising in ten stores, our available stores for ad sales was cut by 20 percent from the outset.

OCTOBER 25, 1991

Our Shopper's Calculators had now been installed in the eight stores for nearly one month; and although we were still awaiting Wal-Mart support data, our advertising sales efforts were underway. As a part of what was to be our very thorough due diligence within Wal-Mart, the first of many-to-follow store manager surveys had been completed. So, in order to showcase the results of these interviews and the associated manager comments, we had our first -– and last -– meeting with Dave Lienemann and his new, but soon-to-depart boss, Rich Donckers, vice president and general merchandise manager for Wal-Mart's Supercenters and Hypermarts. We reviewed the results of our initial store manager interviews with Dave and Rich, and they appeared to be very well received -– as they should have been. Comments from the eight store managers and/or assistant store managers were as follows:

"The response to the Shopper's Calculator program has been great. We have done so many things for our customers that have gone unnoticed. Our customers have definitely noticed the calculators. We have not had one negative comment. Everything has been extremely positive."

Allen Thomas — Hypermart, Kansas City, KS

"Over 60% of our customers are using them. Our customers like to know how much they are spending."

Dan Walters —Hypermart, Topeka, KS

"Everybody thinks the calculators are great. I have personally asked our customers what they think of the calculators and I have had all positive comments. I have even had several customers come find me to tell me how much they like them. I am very enthused about the program."

Paul Gollhofer — Supercenter, Batesville, AR

"Customers love the Shopper's Calculator's. It's a great program."

Greg Epps —Supercenter, Poplar Bluff, MO

"We are very happy with the Shopper's Calculators. Our customers love them."

Gregg Smith —Supercenter, Jefferson City, MO

"Our customers love the Shopper's Calculator program. We are very pleased with the program."

Jon Gardner —Supercenter, Wagoner, OK

"The program is great. We have had lots of positive comments from our customers. Our customers are definitely using them."

Gary Dickens —Supercenter, Wagoner, OK

"We have had lots of customers comment on the program. They all love it."

Jeff Villio — Supercenter, Washington, MO

We again expressed our urgent need for the selling data promised us, and once again our need was acknowledged — but again we left empty-handed.

DECEMBER 4, 1991

For the past five weeks I had placed numerous calls for Dave Lienemann, and left messages on each occasion, expressing our urgent need for their previously promised corporate endorsements and ad sales data — all to no avail.

The questions in-common from every advertising prospect whom we spoke to were: What were the store traffic counts? How many Wal-Mart customers would see their respective ads? Was ours a program in which Wal-Mart truly wanted them to participate? After all, they had heard absolutely nothing from Wal-Mart that would encourage them to participate, and knowing the demands and policies of their respective buyers – even though they liked the sound of our program –– they had to know that their buyers approved of their participation. This was an absolute MUST.

On this day I did reach Lienemann, but again accomplished nothing. Even before I could ask again for the necessary support data, he very quickly told me that he was "far too busy to address that need or to see us at any time within the next three weeks." This was a comment that I was to hear increasingly more often as we continued our Wal-Mart journey. "Being too busy to see us" appeared to be a widespread affliction within the offices of Wal-Mart's management.

In my mind it was apparent that Wal-Mart employed far too many "one-ball jugglers." Give any of them "two balls" or "two projects" and their abilities declined considerably.

However, Lienemann did tell me that he now had a new boss, Jim Donald, vice president of merchandising, and he promised to set a meeting for us with him very soon. Lienemann also stated that the carts in our two uninstalled stores were still without handles; but, he expressed every confidence that they would soon be installed. He also told me that "Wal-Mart continued to be very pleased with the Shopper's Calculator program." To me, it was quite obvious why they would be so pleased. They were enjoying all of the benefits of a new service for their customers and for themselves, and were also being well paid for doing nothing –– not even giving us any part of the assistance that they were contractually bound to provide.

Part II — 1992

Chapter 3
The Games Begin With an Abundance of Promises.

JANUARY 17, 1992

By now it had become all too apparent to our advertising sales force that while our "only game in town" was extremely well-received by Wal-Mart's vendors — and our potential advertisers — we needed either Wal-Mart's endorsement and assistance, or more stores. Eight stores was simply not a legitimate program worthy of any advertiser's consideration. However, the potential for an all-stores Wal-Mart advertising network would be among the most powerful media offerings in the advertising industry, and one in which nearly all of these same advertisers expressed a desire to participate. It was this feedback that prompted me to write a letter to David Glass. Excerpts are as follows:

"As you know, our Shopper's Calculators have now been in your Supercenters and Hypermarts for more than ninety days. Our due diligence with your corporate management, store management and customers indicates that the entire program has been very well received — at every level. Our most recent visits with your store managers have uncovered the following facts — one of which is even a bit unusual. Some of your store managers have letters from customers praising the calculator program. One store manager says his customers have told him they drive extra distances to shop at his Supercenter because of the Shopper's Calculator service. One reports that two of every three

43

of his customers use the calculators. And finally, one initially skeptical store manager took it upon himself to test the units' durability. First he repeatedly threw one against a concrete wall, and then he dropped this same unit in boiling water. To his amazement, the calculator is still working. The bottom line, however, is that they all report that they and their customers are very pleased with the Shopper's Calculators. They all report nothing but positives about the Shopper's Calculators being a meaningful service to Wal-Mart and to its customers.

During the past two years ADDvantage Media has spent in excess of one million dollars for research to document the following: that when used, the Shopper's Calculator is capable of increasing the retailer's customer base, the average transaction size, the sale of advertised products, and the retailer's total sales. This data, coupled with the strong reception of the program in just eight of your stores, makes it apparent that if given the opportunity to roll-out the Shopper's Calculator program throughout all Wal-Mart stores, the advantages to you could be truly awesome.

Kroger has utilized the Shopper's Calculators now for the past 120 days solely to promote their private brand products. Their results have been outstanding. Although they will not share with us the actual increases in private-label sales, they will tell us that the increase in product movement has been 'dramatic', even 'remarkable.' So much so, that they continue to use the calculators solely for the promotion of their own private label products. It would seem that the timing could not be better for Wal-Mart to utilize the Shopper's Calculators in part for promotion of the new Sam's brands and in part to promote the products of Wal-Mart's largest vendors… we would like to discuss a comprehensive Shopper's Calculator program."

Although I followed up by phone on numerous occasions, David Glass proved to be disappointingly consistent. NEVER did he respond to any of my phone calls or letters throughout the course of our seven-year "relationship."

FEBRUARY 25, 1992

Our first and only meeting with Jim Donald, Dave Lienemann's new boss, finally happened. He appeared to be quite pleased with the calculator program and the research associated with it. Although he promised to get involved and assist us, not only with the Supercenter program, but also in achieving a comprehensive Wal-Mart involvement, his lack of effort on our behalf soon became quite apparent. He, too, did not return our phone calls. But, this time it was for a very valid reason. We later learned that he had departed Wal-Mart shortly after being hired.

FEBRUARY 27, 1992

Knowing of our Wal-Mart contract, Peter Childs, a vice president of Merrill Lynch in the Tulsa office, invited me to be his guest to hear David Glass speak to the Friends of Finance Group at a downtown luncheon. It was to be my further good fortune to be seated at a Merrill Lynch table with fellow guest Duane Naccarato, Wal-Mart's regional vice president of operations. Being in my fifth month of frustration with Wal-Mart's –– and Lienemann's –– obvious inability to communicate or make decisions, I seized this opportunity to explain my Wal-Mart predicament and the accompanying frustrations to Duane. As a follow-up to my introduction to Duane and our resulting conversation, I sent him a letter further detailing our current situation with Wal-Mart.

MARCH 2, 1992

Having heard David Glass speak to the Friends of Finance group, and feeling that I really had nothing to lose, I wrote him again, hoping to gain his attention. In this communiqué I stressed the value of our Nielsen research, which found that more than sixty percent of the Wal-Mart customers utilized the calculators on a "frequent" basis. And, 62.7 percent of these same customers stated that they "were able to spend more money on each shopping trip, because they were able to keep track of purchases and not fear spending more monies than they had." But again, this message apparently fell upon deaf ears, as I received absolutely no response.

APRIL 21, 1992

Finally, nearly seven weeks later, we received a sign of having made some progress. What apparently worked was not my additional letter to Glass, but my follow-up letter of explanation and appeal to Duane Naccarato. On this date I received a call from David Burghart, Wal-Mart's vice president of store planning. He asked that we come to Bentonville for a meeting with him and Leroy Rhoades, Wal-Mart's fixture and equipment buyer. Again, one week later, we drove to Bentonville to meet with Burghart and Rhoades. At that meeting we reviewed the research gleaned from our Supercenter program and applied it to a Wal-Mart store-wide program.

The thrust of our presentation was to compare the revenues they were receiving from the present eight-store program with the potential revenues they could receive by including all of their stores — projected to exceed two thousand in the future.

In addition to presenting increased product movement data (which then ranged from eight to 42 percent), we further supported our presentation with more recent store manager testimonials and additional consumer survey data.

The consumer data gleaned from interviews conducted upon the consumers' store exits was perhaps the most convincing, in that it showed that 75 percent of the customers used the calculators to "keep track of their costs/ money spent" — thereby increasing the Wal-Mart store's over-all sales. It further proved that Wal-Mart's customers appreciated and valued the Shopper's Calculator service. When asked to rate the usefulness of the calculator service on a scale of one to five, 43 percent rated it as a "five", 40 percent rated it as a "four" and 17 percent rated it as a "three." No one gave it a rating of a "one" or a "two." We presented the calculator as an opportunity for not just a huge new source of revenue, but one that could simultaneously boost the sales of Wal-Mart's private label products – in particular their line of Sam's Choice beverages. We also discussed the potential of building calculators in a format that was a replica of their Sam's Choice colas, or in the packaged goods format, previously shown on the Shopper's Calculator pictorial page.

APRIL 25, 1992

Less than one week later, David Burghart again contacted me to set a time to meet with him and others for the purpose of further discussing a Wal-Mart/Shopper's Calculator program. He asked that we bring models of our proposed Sam's beverage can calculators and that we also revisit and lower our prices. The latter comment seemed to be the common theme — if not the corporate motto — of Wal-Mart's employees, as we encountered it during the course of nearly every meeting we had with any members of their management team. Their repetitive requests for lowering prices were so prevalent it appeared that "greed" was the sole, driving force behind the company's success.

Comments From Wal-Mart Exit Interviews
Wal-Mart Super Center – Wagoner OK

Use it every time

I like it very much

I love it

I concept – definitely a great improvement for Wal-Mart to offer these calculators

I like them – now I don't have to bring my own

Useful for those who are on fixed budgets

Good idea

Useful for those who use them

Somewhat useful

For those who need them it is useful to have them available

I don't use them – add everything in my head

My wife likes it

Very useful

Using them takes too long

Great service

No time to use it

Men won't use them they just want out of the store

Never use it — I don't like computers

No budget to follow

Helpful – there when you need it

I don't use it to track purchases but I use it to compare which is a better buy

I appreciate the service

I use them all the time – it helps save me money

I use it when I'm doing a lot of shopping

Kids play with it – entertains them

Wish I knew how to use it accurately

I don't have time to use it

Very handy

Great when you want to know how much you have spent

I can't use a calculator correctly

Wal-Mart / Shoppers Calculator Program Benefits

Research has proven that when the customer uses the Shoppers Calculator to track purchases against a budget, she/he spends over 10% more. Nationally 47% of the consumers use the calculator and 62% of these customers use it to track purchases.

In the case of Wal-Mart, 63% of your shoppers use the calculator and 75% use it to track purchases. Therefore, the sales-increasing abilities of each Shoppers Calculator are even more important to Wal-Mart.

Additionally in rating the calculators as a helpful, meaningful service, your existing customer base has given the Shoppers Calculator program an over-all rating of 8.6 on a 10.0 scale.

Finally, this recommended Wal-Mart/ Shoppers Calculator program will provide Wal-Mart with an all new net revenue stream of $15 to $41 million annually.

Wal-Mart / Shoppers Calculator Program Revenue Summary

Depending upon the number of advertisers (12 or 15) and the price per store per cycle ($100 or $150), the total program – currently 1900 stores – will generate between $29.6 million and $55.6 million annually. On a per calculator basis, the annual return ranges between $52 and $97. Obviously as store counts increase the annual revenues will increase accordingly.

Wal-Mart's primary role would be to provide advertiser participation and allow placement of calculators on all shopping carts in all stores for a period of no less than three years.

Wal-Mart / Shoppers Calculator
Annual Advertising Revenue Potential

- <u>Twelve Advertisers</u>
  Comprised of ten national brand advertisers plus two slots for Sam's American Choice Cola brands.
  Thirteen 4-week cycles per advertiser.

  Revenue Potential @ $100/store: $29,640,000
      (Return per calculator: $52)

  Revenue Potential @ $150/store: $44,460,000
      (Return per calculator: $78)

- <u>Fifteen Advertisers</u>
  Comprised of twelve national brand advertisers plus three slots for Sam's American Choice Cola brands.
  Thirteen 4-week cycles per advertiser.

  Revenue Potential @ $100/store: $37,050,000
      (Return per calculator: $65)

  Revenue Potential @ $150/store: $55,575,000
      (Return per calculator: $97.50)

ADDvantage Media Group
Revenue Requirements

ADDvantage Media will:

1. Furnish and install Sam's American Choice Beverage Can Calculators on 20% of all shopping carts and standard Shoppers Calculators on the remaining 80% of all carts in all Wal-Mart retail operations (Wal-Marts, Sam's, Supercenters, Hypermarts, etc.)

2. Service all units on a regular basis.
   Service will consist of cleaning and inspecting all carts/calculators, replacing any damaged or vandalized units, changing all ads for each four-week cycle, replacing damaged or missing ads, etc.

3. Coordinate with advertisers and produce and print all ads for each 4-week advertising schedule.

4. Provide all necessary program management services eliminating the need for any Wal-Mart management or personnel involvement.

IN RETURN, WAL-MART WILL SHARE ADVERTISING REVENUES WITH ADDVANTAGE MEDIA GROUP, INC. AT THE RATE OF $25/CALCULATOR/YEAR, TO BE PAID ON A SCHEDULE COINCIDING WITH EACH 4-WEEK ADVERTISING CYCLE.

Wal-Mart / Shoppers Calculator Program Time Frame and Requirements

ADDvantage Media Needs and Responsibilities:
1. Contract authorization
2. Complete store list with addresses, manager's names, and cart counts by store
3. Make advertising presentations when necessary

Wal-Mart Responsibilities:
1. Provide store lists with cart counts
2. Provide program approval and contract
3. Contact all necessary advertisers/vendors (program to be sold as national advertising – not a promotion)

Upon approval Shoppers Calculator installations would begin within 30 days and continue for approximately seven months. Assuming immediate approval, program could be in place on or prior to January 1. Ad revenues could begin within 90 days of start of installation.

Note: Initially, all carts would be equipped with standard Shoppers Calculators. 20% would be replaced with Sam's American Choice Beverage Can Calculators upon availability. Until that time the designated 20% would carry Sam's American Choice brand ads.

Cost Schedule For Wal-Mart/Shoppers Calculator 3-Year Program

	150,000 Units	300,000 Units	600,000 Units
Program Pricing	$20.05	$19.38	$18.65
(Includes all necessary management time and expenses including (but not limited to) costs of all initial and replacement calculators and installation hardware. Covers cost of all store installations, partial (20%) reinstallations, necessary protective cola can bumpers, and associated freight and taxes. Also includes weekly store visits and comprehensive service — cleaning and maintenance of all units. All necessary expenses — including printing and production coordination — associated with refreshment of the calculator advertising for each 4-week cycle is also included.			
Tooling ($150,000)	1.00	.50	.25
(Can configuration only)			
Required Cost Per Calculator Per Year	$21.05	$19.88	$18.90
Less 5% Annual Cart Shrinkage Service Allowance	(1.00)	(.97)	(.93)
Net Cost Per Calculator Per Year	$20.05	$18.91	$17.97

"The success of Sam's American Choice will be short-term — Long term, Sam's Choice will go down the tubes. — Sam's Choice in the long run will never generate more than 5% or 10% of the business."

Advertising Age, April 27, 1992

"Not Necessarily"

Shoppers Calculator
May 19, 1992

Chapter 4

It's Been a Year, Our First Payment is Due, and We Are Threatened for the First Time.

MAY 19, 1992

Frank Jerd, our executive vice president of sales, joined me this day as we drove to Bentonville to again present our calculator concept. But this time we were excited. We were to meet with not just David Burghart, but for the first time, we were actually going to meet with two of Wal-Mart's advertising executives, Bob McCurry and Barbara Brown. We left this meeting charged with drafting a contract that accurately represented the conclusions that had emerged from our discussions. Although we had reduced our per unit pricing from twenty-five dollars to twenty dollars, this group of Wal-Mart executives once again instructed us to reduce it -- this time to "our lowest possible pricing level," which became $17.97. This was a tough assignment, but they finally appeared to be ready to sign a contract and fortunately, we still had a "decent" profit margin built into this price point. However, had we not been forewarned of the price-cutting demands that were a mandatory part of every Wal-Mart opportunity, we could have been in serious trouble. Two days later we delivered the contract, further revised as they had requested.

JUNE 24, 1992

We placed numerous follow-up phone calls over the next few weeks, all to no avail. Then, finally after a period of three weeks since our last meeting with Burghart, McCurry and Brown, David Burghart called to schedule a meeting for June 24. He described this meeting as being "our final contract discussions" prior to initiating a Wal-Mart/Shopper's Calculator program. At this meeting we were presented with the changes requested by Wal-Mart's legal department — all of which were simply boilerplate in nature. But, after reviewing these changes, they AGAIN requested an additional price reduction, and being so close, we again conceded. We returned to Tulsa, and on the next day the revised contracts incorporating Wal-Mart's legal department changes, as well as the new pricing, were delivered to Wal-Mart.

Since we had been told that the only remaining factor was the actual signing of the final revised contract, we left this meeting to meet with Dave Lienemann to discuss folding our initial Supercenter/Hypermart agreement into the latest Wal-Mart contract. According to Lienemann, this was a decision that he could not make, and he would get back to us in the very near future.

However, near the end of this meeting we did have a rather alarming conversation with Lienemann. Just as we were about to leave his office he made the remark, "**You know that if we like what these calculators do for our business, we might just start making our own.**"

My response was simply, "We are protected by fourteen patents. The only way to circumvent them would be to hang a calculator off of the shopping cart with a string or a wire."

His response definitely got my attention, as he told me: "So what? You don't have the money or the power to go up against Wal-Mart in an Arkansas courtroom."

This was to be the first time that I truly experienced what supposedly was a part of Sam's early business philosophy: "our goal is to own you or destroy you."

This conversation turned out to be very prophetic, but believe me it was more than scary at the time these statements were made. And, from my prospective, such actions had to be on someone's mind(s), otherwise there was no reason for them to be made.

Although it was most apparent that we were making no progress, contractually we were now obligated to make our initial payment to Wal-Mart for the eight stores in which we were installed. And, because we were not about to give anyone any reason to terminate our contract, we issued this first check in the amount of $16,000 — for what appeared to be solely the "privilege" of having our products in too few of their stores.

Thereafter we remained hopeful that this payment, despite their non-performance, would further our cause in obtaining a workable Wal-Mart agreement. The very next day we also returned the contract, which contained all of the changes requested by their in-house counsel, as well as Wal-Mart's further-negotiated pricing. One year had now passed, but it appeared that we and Wal-Mart were FINAL-LY ready to launch a meaningful program.

Chapter 5

We Tried to Join Sam's Club.

JULY 8, 1992

Confident of having both our Wal-Mart and Wal-Mart Supercenter/Hypermart programs virtually in our pocket, Frank Jerd, our EVP Sales, and I initiated a selling effort across the street from Wal-Mart's corporate headquarters, at Sam's Club. We had an appointment to meet with Jeff Crabtree, the Sam's Club manager of "other income." We had been told by Wal-Mart personnel that he was the person to see, for our program appeared to be precisely the type that Jeff, too, would be seeking. So, naturally, our next step was to visit the corporate offices of Sam's Club.

This visit was unique from the outset. The Sam's Club headquarters featured an unfinished cinder-block exterior which had the aesthetic appeal of a small child's LEGO building project. The interior was constructed from white pine. Furthermore, this sparse interior, in combination with the picnic tables that functioned as conference tables gave the impression of a roughly hewn hunting lodge situated in the backwoods of Canada.

No sooner had we entered the front door, than we were asked to hang up our coats and ties in their designated cloakroom. It mattered not who you were there to see, all visitors were required to remove their ties and strip down to just shirts and slacks. Even today, I am not really certain of the reasons behind such requests, but can only assume that it was because no one on the Sam's side was dressed up. The Sam's corporate uniforms all appeared to have been purchased from Sam's. Nearly everyone was wearing the very least-expensive polyester shirts and pants. Evidently this policy was to put everyone on an equal footing should there be any pricing negotiations.

Our invitation to take a seat at the picnic table within our assigned 8 by12-foot conference room seemed to fit right in with their overall scheme of things. Austerity apparently led to even lower prices. At least that appeared to be the intent of the decorator.

Our initial presentation to Jeff was an overlay of the proposal that had been accepted for the Wal-Mart stores. However, we also offered the option –– previously offered, but by-passed by Wal-Mart –– of paying Sam's Club on a per-cart basis. It was this latter approach that Jeff found to be the most appealing. He said that he would discuss our proposal with his bosses. Per Jeff, he was seeking revenue-generating programs like ours, but it was imperative that they not usurp any part of the revenue streams currently being generated from the majority of their vendors. Furthermore, any such programs must not, in any way, impact their vendors' pricing structures to them.

We left this meeting truly on a "high." Our thoughts and visions of a genuine, all-inclusive program were now complete. The Shopper's Calculator program included not just the Wal-Mart stores, their Supercenters and Hypermarts, but now there appeared to be a strong possibility that the Sam's Club outlets would also join our network.

The very next day, all of our Wal-Mart dreams were shattered. When I answered a phone call from David Burghart, for what I anticipated to be a confirmation of the contract signing date, I was told that the Shopper's Calculator program had been "suspended." He further advised me that this action was at the direction of Paul Higham (pronounced high -am), Wal-Mart's then vice president of advertising. He further told us that: "Higham is of the opinion that your solicitation of Wal-Mart's vendors for monies to support the Shopper's Calculator program would quite possibly jeopardize Wal-Mart's existing sources for promotional funds. Furthermore it could very possibly influence Wal-Mart's future cost of goods."

This action was taken despite our assurances of making all of our ad sales calls solely on the people responsible for the national advertising budgets of Wal-Mart's vendors — and never on those persons responsible for the "special promotional funds" reserved for support of product sales within the mass merchant outlets.

My thirty years in the advertising agency business had provided me with an incredible amount of insight into the working mechanics of special promotional funds — especially from the varying viewpoints of the manufacturers and the retailers.

I had previously made numerous trips to the buying offices of the major mass merchants — including Wal-Mart and Kmart — accompanying my clients for the sole purpose of presenting the future year's ad campaign to each client's respective buyers. Without exception, at each of these meetings, following the presentation of the client's forthcoming ad campaign — to assure the buyer that the client was indeed supporting the potential sales of its product line — the promotional funds discussions ensued. In each case the buyer's pitch was his need for additional promotional funds in order to place my client's products in ads on television, in newspapers, in their respective inserts, mailers, etc., and in each case they assured the client of major coverage via all media.

The client then committed to giving the buyers "x" dollars in order to do so, knowing that if they did not subscribe to the buyer's requests, their products would never be promoted beyond the price point sign on the shelf. In fact, they would be quite fortunate if their product line was ever again carried in the years to come.

But this was never the end of the buyer's solicitation for his "necessary" promotional funds. Several times throughout each year the buyer would call back seeking additional funds in order to place the client's product or products within a special promotion. If the client even hesitated to respond, the veiled threat of their competitor's willingness to participate was always a part of the buyer's presentation. Consequently, rarely did a vendor decline to assist his buyer with his need for additional promotional dollars.

On certain occasions, a portion of these special promotional funds was used to purchase support media, but more often than not, these dollars went straight to the mass merchant's bank account. These "contributions" allowed the buyer to further lower the price points of the previously selected promotional products, thus allowing the retailer to further promote their "falling prices" to the consuming public.

The good news was that there was never a co-mingling of the dollars committed to national advertising and the dollars budgeted for these special promotional funds. Quite often the vendors' promotional funds -- allocated in specific amounts for specific retailers -- were re-allocated from one retailer to another, in order to accommodate a specific retailer's demands. But I never witnessed any funds being removed from a national advertising budget in order to accommodate these same retailer demands.

It was our sole intent to call upon only those "pockets" responsible for funding the national advertising campaigns -- either the product's manufacturer or the advertising agencies responsible for their client's national advertising campaigns. And the advertising on the calculators was to be used solely as a point of purchase reminder in support of the product's national ad campaign.

Our depth of understanding of how the "special promotional funds" system functioned, in combination with our past advertising clients telling us that "**Wal-Mart and AD-Dvantage Media impact totally separate departments, separate people and separate budgets — with zero crossover in any area,**" led me to seek a higher court of appeal — one that hopefully also understood this system. Because we had previously been told that Bill Fields, Wal-Mart's executive vice president of merchandise and sales, had been supportive of our program, I elected to direct my initial letter of appeal to him.

We made repeated attempts to reach Fields by phone, but all efforts were unsuccessful and our messages went unanswered. However, less than two weeks after mailing our letter to Fields, we were contacted by Bob McCurry, a member of Wal-Mart's advertising department with whom we had previously met. He asked that we return to Wal-Mart to again visit with him and Matt Loveless of their advertising department.

Although Bob was unable to attend this meeting, we did have our first meeting with the young and enthusiastic Matt Loveless. His opening remarks told us that Bill Fields had personally appointed him to be our liaison and although he had not been involved previously, it was his intent to immediately get up to speed. Even though he appeared to be a newly hired trainee, he was very believable. Accordingly, we believed that he would do everything in his power to assist us. Unfortunately, it did not take long to discover that he was virtually powerless.

Matt did tell us that Wal-Mart no longer had any interest in selling the program, but instead was now interested in the potential of ADDvantage Media selling the program on Wal-Mart's behalf. However, in advance of a final decision of this nature, he wished to see a revised contract and requested that a sixty-day test be conducted in Wal-Mart's newest store, the Bentonville Supercenter. By doing so, the Shopper's Calculators and the Wal-Mart private-label product ads could and would be viewed by all members of Wal-Mart's management team.

Simultaneously, Wal-Mart could conduct additional research to verify the research that ADDvantage Media had previously conducted. Additionally, it was Wal-Mart's then-stated intent to use the calculators to advertise their private-label products. By doing so, they could further test the product movement abilities of the Shopper's Calculators.

Having little choice, we once again accepted their terms. But, it was quite difficult since the terms of the newly proposed contract called for no less than 200 stores, as opposed to the more than 1900 stores specified in the contract of two weeks ago.

Chapter 6

Another Year, Another Payment, and They Want Yet Another Test.

AUGUST 10, 1992

Another year had now passed since we initiated the testing of our products in Wal-Mart's appointed stores. We continued to be restricted to eight of our ten contractually specified stores because the cart handles had still not been replaced in the remaining two stores, Furthermore, our greatest needs continued to be their in-store marketing data and their supportive endorsement. **We had yet to receive any of either, yet another $16,000 payment was due to Wal-Mart.**

But, it appeared that we were making some progress, for we were now to meet with Matt Loveless for him to outline the structure of the "**one final test**" that stood between us and a chain-wide program. This test was to be conducted in the Bentonville Supercenter – their newest Supercenter, and in theory, a prototype for the future. But, perhaps of greatest importance to us was the fact that our Shopper's Calculators would be in their newest store, in Bentonville, where all of Wal-Mart's management to see and utilize our Shopper's Calculators.

The purpose of this meeting was to discuss the specific products that Wal-Mart wished to promote and test during the forthcoming sixty-day test. Also, because it was intended that ADDvantage Media would sell the advertising for the future program, we discussed at length the need for us to be given Wal-Mart's marketing statistics, inclusive of average weekly transactions, customer counts, etc.

We also needed to know the products that Wal-Mart intended to promote on the calculators -— for testing purposes -— along with the necessary art for printing these product ads, and just how Wal-Mart intended to conduct its research in order to judge the effectiveness of the program.

It wasn't the latter that we were concerned with, as **numerous previous tests had already proven the calculators to be the most effective in-store advertising media available.** However if the test was to be conducted over the forthcoming sixty days, the advertising materials (ads) needed to be printed immediately, and it was also imperative that we be given their marketing data for our selling purposes. We also discussed our preferred dates for installation, as well as our need of their permission to employ hostesses to introduce the calculators to Wal-Mart's shoppers.

We exited this meeting leaving behind a cover letter of explanation and a revised contract (which reflected each of their requested changes) for review by Bob McCurry and other members of Wal-Mart's management.

For the ensuing six weeks, in advance of our planned installation of the Bentonville Supercenter, as instructed, we channeled all of our communications through Matt Loveless. He proved to be very cooperative. However, like so many of the Wal-Mart employees we had been asked to deal with, he had no authority, and he continued to be unable to obtain or provide us with any helpful information.

Although we repeatedly asked for the advertising art for the products to be tested, the only messages that were approved were our utilization of Wal-Mart's slogans "We're Rolling Up Our Sleeves, And Rolling Back Prices" and "Always the Lowest Prices On The Brands You Trust — Always."

As a result, when we installed the Bentonville store there were no product messages on any of the Shopper's Calculators. The calculators contained only our "How to Use" instructional inserts plus the two Wal-Mart slogans previously mentioned.

On a near-daily basis, we continued to press for answers concerning both our need for Wal-Mart's marketing data and art that would allow us to print the private-label product ads that were to be used for testing purposes. We continued to receive no answers, despite Matt continuing to tell us that Wal-Mart managers all "absolutely loved the program," and in particular, Bill Fields.

As further evidence to such opinions, Wal-Mart's store managers continued to rave about the program and many others requested that their respective stores be installed – despite their being located in areas not specified as part of the test.

On the strength of these positive comments and the continuing potential of our Wal-Mart program, ADDvantage Media's management and directors borrowed and personally guaranteed several hundred thousand additional dollars to further fund this "final" test.

Throughout the time Wal-Mart was conducting its final sixty-day test in the Bentonville Supercenter, we continued to ask for test objectives and marketing data. Although we received none, we continued to have our seven national ad salesmen as well as our entire management team make sales calls, focusing on the national ad budgets of the Wal-Mart vendors. The latter was the easiest part of the test.

Almost without exception, Wal-Mart's vendors saw the potential of such a media network, within Wal-Mart, as being an outstanding media opportunity. It was hailed as one that could supplant traditional media advertising. Some looked at it as an entirely new medium, so targeted that it could influence the sale of their products in every store.

It was hardly a surprise when our Supercenter/Hypermart agreement was suspended pending the results of Wal-Mart's final test. Almost immediately thereafter we were told that the Sam's Club management had also elected to defer its decision.

Having done business in the past with over 100 of Wal-Mart's vendors, while our Shopper's Calculators were installed in grocery stores, it was not a difficult sell to convince these same advertisers of the merits of a Wal-Mart program. Essentially, two things stood in our way to selling out the entire program — a chain-wide contract with Wal-Mart and a roll-out schedule as to when all stores would be installed. Beyond that, it appeared to be a matter of assigning cycle dates, finalizing rates and getting contracts out for signatures.

The response from advertisers was so very positive that we continued to request that Wal-Mart provide us with a representative to verify the fact that we were on the brink of having a chain-wide Wal-Mart in-store advertising program. We further verified — to ourselves and to Wal-Mart — that the dollars that advertisers anticipated spending on the Wal-Mart in-store program would be an all-new source of revenue for Wal-Mart and not just a shifting of dollars already being "given" to Wal-Mart in the form of "special promotional dollars." They would be coming from the national advertising budgets of their vendors and therefore were dollars never-before accessed by Wal-Mart, despite their past, repeated efforts to do so.

The bottom line, with few exceptions, was that national advertisers saw a Wal-Mart/Shopper's Calculator program as one with potentially huge impact on their future product sales within the Wal-Mart stores and in the minds of consumers wherever they shopped. The fact that each Wal-Mart consumer would be exposed to their advertised product for twenty-five minutes or more — during the typical shopping trip — was an ad exposure unlike any other. This was a huge added value.

Simultaneously, the program promised to generate millions of dollars worth of new revenues for Wal-Mart and our company. From Wal-Mart's perspective it was not merely a no-lose program, but an absolute no-brainer. They would obtain millions of dollars in new revenues, provide their customers with an immensely popular service, and increase sales per transaction, as well as the sales of the advertised products. The entire program would cost Wal-Mart nothing. The advertisers would shoulder the entire cost of the program.

Although our latest agreement called for our Wal-Mart Bentonville test to expire on November 15, we were unsuccessful in even obtaining a meeting with Wal-Mart until after the first of the New Year. On December 8, we were finally able to speak with Bob McCurry and establish a time for a meeting to discuss the results of the Bentonville store test. However, it was readily apparent that no test had ever been conducted. Consequently, in advance of our meeting, scheduled for 2 p.m. on January 5, we sent a letter to Bob McCurry addressing our concerns.

But, the good news during this significant time lapse was the positive reports given to us by all of our sales representatives. Without exception, they each validated a "great deal of enthusiasm" that was being exhibited by nearly all of their clients for the forthcoming Wal-Mart program. During this time our home office received many calls from Wal-Mart store managers, each of whom requested information on how to become a part of the Shopper's Calculator program. In all cases our phone number had been given to them by one of the eight managers of the presently participating stores.

Part III — 1993

Chapter 7
More and More Unfulfilled Promises.

JANUARY 8, 1993

After a very-frustrating eighteen months of unanswered correspondence, unfulfilled promises, program starts-and-stops, and meeting postponements, we were to have what we deemed to be the long-awaited and all-important meeting with Bob McCurry and other members of the Wal-Mart management team. We truly believed that this time we would be allowed to discuss the future of the Shopper's Calculator/Wal-Mart program.

We had completed what had been "billed" as our final test, and although we knew that no actual test was ever conducted our regular and thorough interviews with the Bentonville store personnel gave us every reason to believe that we had passed this test with absolutely flying colors. In not one interview with this store's employees had we been given a single negative. According to Matt, the program was "loved by all."

But, on the day of this all-important meeting, to our great disappointment again, the only Wal-Mart "executive" available was Matt Loveless. As always, he apologized for the lack of other Wal-Mart personnel in the meeting and he did review with us the consumer research that Wal-Mart had conducted during the time of the Bentonville test.

Surprisingly Wal-Mart had conducted some research. It was nothing compared to the intentions outlined to us at the outset of this final test, but they had supposedly conducted more than one thousand additional customer interviews. We were told that their results were virtually an overlay of the results gleaned from our nearly five thousand interviews in the past. Sixty-three percent of Wal-Mart's customers used the calculators and 75 percent of these same customers used them to track purchases.

On a scale of one to ten, the customers in this Wal-Mart study rated the service as an 8.5. This number compared to the 8.6 rating of our Nielsen Company research. But 8.5 was still most impressive, considering the fact that it was Wal-Mart's own number, and therefore should not lack any credibility.

Overall it was extremely comforting to know that their research was virtually the same as ours, given the far lesser sample (of Wal-Mart customers) and the fact that it was conducted by Wal-Mart employees, not research professionals.

We presented a new proposal for the Wal-Mart/ Shopper's Calculator program. This one was based entirely upon ADDvantage Media selling the advertising. We left behind all details of the proposed program and followed up with a letter to Loveless to further explain and document this proposal. Being obviously embarrassed by the lack of attendance for our scheduled meeting, Loveless promised to again establish a meeting date (convenient to Wal-Mart's executives) and do so in the near future.

The following week, Loveless issued an in-house memorandum to Wal-Mart's management outlining the mechanics of our newly proposed program, as he saw it. He also included the results of Wal-Mart's more than one thousand exit interviews at the Bentonville store. Matt's attempt to communicate all aspects of our program was riddled with errors and incomplete thoughts. For example, his memo stated that ADDvantage Media would share all revenues in excess of "$100,000 per unit." The actual figure should have been in excess of one hundred dollars. He also quite erroneously stated, "Kmart would determine whether or not they would participate in the Shopper's Calculator program based upon Wal-Mart's decision." There was no correlation between the two, and aside from being up-front and advising him that Kmart was testing our program, this had never been discussed.

Immediately, I called each of these errors to Matt's attention, and then faxed him all necessary changes. But, a corrected memorandum was never issued.

FEBRUARY 5, 1993

Prior to this date, Matt Loveless again called us to say that our much-anticipated meeting had now been set for February 5. This time he assured us that Wal-Mart executives would be present and they would include Bill Fields, Paul Higham and a few other members of their advertising and marketing hierarchy.

Upon our arrival in Bentonville, however, we faced still another disappointment. Matt Loveless was again present, and with him was another advertising staffer, Barbara Brown, but none of the others that we had been told would be in attendance.

Despite the absence of Fields and Higham, we were told that Wal-Mart had elected to rollout the program and was finally in the process of determining quantities and locations of stores to be included in the program. Wal-Mart also wanted to proceed with our "packaged goods concept," replicating the Sam's Choice beverage-can calculators, but had not yet determined the number of units to be allocated per store.

At this meeting we also reiterated the fact that the Michigan Wal-Mart store, which had previously requested the installation of our calculators — but had been turned down awaiting the conclusion of the test — should be contacted and/or considered as a candidate for installation.

FEBRUARY 8, 1993

The day we had awaited for more than eighteen months finally occurred. Matt Loveless called to say that although the final number of stores and locations had not yet been finalized, the program was otherwise at a point of "all systems go."

In accordance with this news, letters of thanks were sent to both Bill Fields and Matt Loveless. It was apparent that the millions of dollars invested in the program, coupled with the additional $275,000 that management had recently personally funded, had not been spent in vain and would soon begin to reap big dividends.

Based upon the verbal commitments of Brown and Loveless, in conjunction with the continued very positive feedback from our future in-store advertising participants, we elected to de-install our grocery store network in preparation for our forthcoming Wal-Mart/mass-merchant network. Putting all of our eggs, and our future, in Wal-Mart's baskets made dollars and sense. Obviously, selling advertising for Sam Walton's Wal-Mart stores held far greater revenue potential than the previously installed neighborhood grocery store chains.

FEBRUARY 11, 1993

Matt Loveless called, this time to tell us that Paul Higham — whom we had still not met, or been able to speak with —had again reversed Wal-Mart's previous decision to implement our program. Loveless was not aware of what had prompted him to do so this time, nor did he know any of Higham's reasons for doing so. He only knew that this decision had been made solely by Paul Higham. Having already borrowed more money and initiated the necessary steps to implement the program, we immediately wrote and placed phone calls to Higham and Fields. Predictably, these actions were to no avail, as neither responded to our calls or follow-up letters of appeal.

FEBRUARY 16, 1993

Fortunately, but only by accident, I was able to reach Paul Higham by phone. Obviously, his secretary had left her desk, and only after I let his phone ring twenty-plus times, did Higham answer.

I reiterated our shock and queried the reasons for asking us to conduct an eighteen-month test if they had no intention of installing the program.

Perhaps because of this accusation, Higham agreed to meet with us the following week. Accordingly, we composed a letter summarizing our position and mailed it to him in advance of this forthcoming meeting. We then began to plan our strategy for how we could best take advantage of our meeting with this "invisible man," one whom we'd never met, but the one who appeared to be our most outspoken opponent — from behind the scenes.

Chapter 8

We Finally Meet Our Invisible Adversary.

FEBRUARY 24, 1993

On this date, our CFO, Gary Young, accompanied me on the trip to Bentonville. We were beginning to believe that Bill Fields did not really exist, or at least he appeared to be a figment of Loveless's imagination. Again we had been told that he would be present for this meeting. He was not, but Paul Higham and Barbara Brown were.

cAlthough I felt like I should know Higham, based upon the many references to him in prior meetings, we had not previously had any personal encounters. Accordingly, my initial and immediate impression was that he was one of the very few islands in Wal-Mart's sea of "polyester people."

He was dapperly attired, his hair was combed straight back, and he wore an "all-business" facial expression. That said, it too was obvious that he wore his ego on his monogrammed cuffs.

It was also readily apparent that he had been opposed to our program since day one, despite having authorized his key and subordinate personnel, Bob McCurry and Barbara Brown, to meet and negotiate with us for more than nine months. Whether this lack of coordination within his department was simply a common occurrence of the left hand not knowing what the right hand was doing, or Paul Higham truly had somewhat of a vendetta against us, stemming from our entering David Glass's office first, as opposed to his — this we could not determine. But, it was readily apparent that he was much brighter than his actions — which we had witnessed from afar — had led us to believe.

We again reviewed the results of all of our in-store testing, which had been compiled over a time-frame now exceeding eighteen months. We also presented a detailed explanation of each of the elements of our proposed program, highlighting the opinions of both his customers and the potential program advertisers.

In strong contrast to Sam Walton's stated philosophy of "the customer being number one," Higham's response was that he "could care less what his customers thought about the value of the calculator service." His only concern was "whether or not it would truly generate new revenues for the company without impacting their 'everyday low pricing' in any way." He further and rather emphatically told us that "Wal-Mart could sell its vendors anything they wanted to, and they certainly did not need anyone's help to do so."

This said, he proceeded to listen intently as we reviewed the opportunity to secure an all-new revenue stream from his vendors' national advertising departments and their respective advertising agencies. During this discussion, we detailed the very positive results of our more than one-year's worth of ad sales calls on Wal-Mart's behalf.

Higham also appeared to be fascinated by the potential application of our packaged-goods concept, as it could apply to advertised products, but not as it would apply to the Sam's Choice beverage program.

In fact, he appeared to be so infatuated with this concept, that we left him all photos and hand-crafted models (approximately ten thousand dollars worth of prototypes). Despite our multiple requests for their re-

turn, we were never to see them again, and no explanation was ever given as to their whereabouts or fate.

During the course of this meeting, we further queried Higham as to why we had received so many positive reports from Loveless attesting to the success of our program and the accompanying management approval.

He had no answer. However, he did say that Loveless's reports of Fields praising the program had to be erroneous. As he further stated, "I don't believe Loveless has ever had a conversation with Fields, much less any meetings."

Despite the aloof and sarcastic demeanor Higham had displayed at the outset of our meeting, he became most gracious and apparently much more understanding towards its end. It was difficult to know just what he did and did not understand about the merits of our program. But, he promised to look into it and "get back with us."

He was also courteous enough to walk Gary Young and me to the front door of their corporate headquarters. However, during the course of this walk together, he specifically advised us that "had we been smart enough to see him first on this program, he could have made it a lot easier for us." My response was that David Glass had not given me a road map, but had I been aware of Higham and his feelings, I would have made every effort to travel the "Higham Highway." David Glass would have been second on my list. And had I been given the opportunity to employ hindsight, Glass would have been at the absolute bottom.

Coincidentally, Gene Bay, our New York sales consultant, faxed me on this same day to say that five of the advertising agencies for Procter & Gamble were going to, or had already recommended that P&G utilize the Shopper's Calculator program to reach its Wal-Mart customers. The five brands included Gain, Joy, Sure, Pringles and Gillette.

MARCH 8, 1993

After attempting to reach Higham for nearly one week, and again having none of my phone calls returned, I began to call him at all hours of the day and night in hopes that I might be able to catch him when only he was there to answer his phone.

This strategy paid off. I was able to catch him in his office very early this particular morning, obviously prior to the arrival of his secretary. Higham told me that his "buyers were unwilling to mess with selling any advertising for the calculators." This response was contrary to the entire focus of the meeting we just had with him, at which time it was determined that ADDvantage Media would sell the advertising for Wal-Mart, and in so doing, access millions of dollars in new revenues. These would be dollars that their buyers would never be able to access, as they would come from the national advertising dollars within their vendors' budgets.

Though he seemed to be very bright, it was readily apparent that he had missed the entire point of our previous meeting. Then again, this comment may have been made by our program's leading adversary, solely for my benefit

When asked what testing had been done in the Bentonville store, as it related to sales increases, he replied "None." When I further queried him as to whether they had compared revenues of the eight Supercenters in which the calculators were installed, with the revenues of eight comparable Supercenters having no calculators, he simply advised me that: " I do not know what tests have been conducted," nor did he know "if any results had been determined." He appeared to be unknowing, and showed no sign of being willing to cooperate with us in any way, **whatsoever.**

Chapter 9

"Neighborliness and Honesty" Are Not a Part of Today's "Wal-Mart Way."

MARCH 31, 1993

Five weeks and too many unreturned phone calls later, I contacted Higham by letter. I pointed out that, "I recognized that decision processes take time. But it appears that our patience, full cooperation, and willingness to continue to invest heavily — now for more than eighteen months — have been rewarded only with delays, changes in direction and overall non-responsiveness at every turn. When we compare our previous instructions from Wal-Mart with the future direction you outlined in our last meeting, we've been grievously misled in the past."

For the past eighteen months we had done all they had asked, and more. We were offering Wal-Mart a no-lose program worth millions of dollars and Higham was continuing to ignore us — and apparently enjoying doing so.

The bottom line appeared to be that we were spending ourselves into bankruptcy while traveling Higham's "highway to nowhere." As a result, I sent an additional letter to Higham in hopes of politely alerting him to each of these facts.

APRIL 11, 1993

I received Higham's letter of response, dated April 6, telling me, "I know it must be frustrating waiting. Please be patient." It had been nearly five months since completion of the "final" sixty-day Bentonville test. All had and continued to go well in the stores and with their customers and their respective managers. Yet the testing continued and both our patience and our costs of doing business were not just being "tested," but were being pushed well beyond any reasonable limits.

APRIL 28, 1993

This was a day of two big surprises. Steve Hunter of the Wal-Mart finance department contacted me to further discuss our contract, and we received a letter from Higham stating that he had elected to install our calculators in two hundred stores — not the one thousand nine hundred stores committed in the initial contract.

Wal-Mart, or more than likely, solely Higham, had now elected to have their buyers solicit the monies to support our program. This made absolutely no sense. This action was contrary to everything we had been told and charged to prove for the past eighteen months. The buyers reportedly had already said that "they did not want to mess with selling it." That was because they knew they would never be allowed to even touch the all-important new stream of revenue from the national advertising budgets. We had already proven time and again that we could be very successful in doing so.

It was readily apparent that Higham, in asking the buyers to sell the program, had further engineered the death of our program. His letter stated that "while we remain somewhat wary of this concept, we feel that further study is necessary." This proved an interesting summation, since they had now been "testing" our program for nearly two years. Finally, he advised us that Loveless and Brown were now to be our contacts.

MAY 5, 1993

For the very first time since the outset of our relationship, Paul Higham actually accepted my phone call. I had called to thank him for the opportunity to further our Shopper's Calculator program, but more importantly to question the wisdom of having his buyers — "who did not want to mess with our program" — attempt to sell it. I also requested that I be able to have a follow-up meeting with him in the near future. He abruptly apprised me that he "would be too busy to have any further meetings" with me, but the program had been initiated and I was to work through Loveless in the future.

Upon completion of my conversation with Higham, I immediately called Loveless to further determine the status of the program. He advised me that the Wal-Mart buyers had already initiated their selling process for the program and that he needed the contract returned to him as quickly as possible. The contract was sent via Federal Express, that same day, to Loveless, Brown, and Higham.

MAY 12, 1993

On this date, Loveless advised me that the contract had been received and was in legal for approval. He further wanted an assurance that we would be able to have units installed by September 1, 1993. I confirmed this date, assuming the contract would be signed in the immediate future. Loveless expressed confidence that it would be, as it had already been reviewed by the advertising and marketing personnel and was in legal for final approval.

MAY 25, 1993

As of this date we still did not have a signed contract. Loveless confirmed that the contract was still on Higham's desk, awaiting his signature. I again reinforced our need to have a signed contract. We could not initiate the manufacturing of the necessary quantity of units until all parties had agreed to terms, as outlined in the contract.

Chapter 10

Apparently Common Courtesy Has No Place in Their Business Methodology.

JUNE 5, 1993

One more time we attempted to determine the status of the contract. Loveless again told us that the contract was still on Higham's desk, awaiting his signature. It was simply too apparent that Higham's earlier statement to me that he was "just too busy" to meet with me carried over to anything and everything that was related to the Shopper's Calculator program.

But, Loveless also gave us some good news. He told us that of all the advertisers that the Wal-Mart buyers had contacted, only one had declined, and the responses from the others had been quite positive. Although the store list had still not been determined, Loveless remained confident that the number of stores would exceed the two hundred outlined in the contract. On this same date, Loveless faxed us the other changes that Higham had now stipulated to be added to the contract. He wanted these additional stipulations written into it:

(1)   Only Wal-Mart's buyers would be allowed to solicit funding for this advertising program.

(2)   The calculators will be rolled-out to stores only as sponsorship funding is found by the buyers.

(3) All announcements, of public nature, of this further test will be approved by Wal-Mart.

(4) The sole factor for final approval will be the judgment of the Wal-Mart buyers as to whether or not the cost of advertising on the calculators will have a negative effect on the cost of goods.

It was obvious that Higham's newest stipulation that "the buyers would be the sole factor for approval" was his way of further writing in an "out." However, the contract still contained a best-efforts clause, and we continued to be convinced that once Wal-Mart truly tried it, they would have to like it — with or without a blessing from Higham.

On June 9, the contract was returned to Wal-Mart with each of these revisions in place. On this same date, Loveless requested that we provide Wal-Mart with a flyer for their buyers to use in selling the advertising. This was a bit surprising, for on May 5, we had been told that the selling process had already been initiated and was going extremely well — without the need for a flyer,

JUNE 15, 1993

Now, more than two months after Higham had agreed to terms, we still did not have a signed contract. Despite this restrictive detail, we continued to expend monies to maintain the program in the Supercenters in anticipation of a signed Wal-Mart agreement and a full Supercenter program.

Although we continued to request meetings and ask that they return a signed contract, Loveless advised me that Wal-Mart — and Higham — did not wish to schedule any meetings at this time.

Loveless also asked that we provide him with a list of all of the ad agencies and national advertisers whom we had contacted during the past eighteen months. He advised me that they intended to sell the program to each advertiser for $20,000 per ad cycle. This statement confused us even more since this would make the program merely self-liquidating and not one capable of generating the additional revenues they sought at every turn. Furthermore they had failed to build in any discounts for multiple cycles, etc.

Now more than ever, it was too apparent that either they did not know how to go about selling an in-store program or, as we continued to suspect, they had no intention of doing so.

Two days later, we provided Loveless with a letter to advertisers, a sales flyer outlining all aspects of the program and its selling benefits, a proposed news release announcing the program, and a list of all advertisers we had previously contacted on Wal-Mart's behalf.

JUNE 22, 1993

For the following two weeks we continued to have nearly daily dialogue with Loveless, each time requesting the store list, the approved news release, and a signed contract. Each time we were told that they were all in the works, and that Higham continued to be "extremely busy," etc.

I also counseled with Matt that he not allow advertisers to "cherry-pick" prime promotional months, holidays, etc. I further advised him that he needed to structure his program pricing so that it was profitable and also allowed for discounts that provided incentives for multiple and long-term advertiser commitments.

On June 30, nearly two months later, Higham's busy schedule slackened sufficiently for him to sign the contract and return it to us.

JULY 8, 1993

More than three weeks after we first supplied Wal-Mart with our proposed news release, we still had no approval. We continued to make requests of Wal-Mart for their approval, knowing that the longer this process took, the more in violation of SEC regulations we were — being a public company. Finally, on July 14, the release was approved, precisely as submitted one month prior.

On the strength of this new, "signed" Wal-Mart contract, we were now able to obtain an additional bank loan for three hundred and twenty-five thousand dollars. These were the monies necessary to pay a portion of our long-overdue payables and to put our company in a position to initiate making the store installations.

The nearly two years of testing had taken a heavy toll on not just our people, but on our finances and the stock market value of our company. You can only shout "wolf" so many times, and in this case, our doing so for nearly two years seriously damaged our personal and corporate credibility.

This was a fact of life to which our Wal-Mart contacts were wholly oblivious. But, why should they worry? As we had been told by too many Wal-Mart employees, on too many occasions, they owned so much Wal-Mart stock that they were all nearly independently wealthy. They may have been, but it was apparent they were not getting rich due to their intellects or because they were adhering to any of Sam's past-stated values.

My observations told me that most were accumulating their wealth by saving their clothing allowances, and in a few cases, by saving on personal laundering expenses, too.

But what was far too obvious was the fact that we were the ones being "taken to the cleaners."

JULY 20, 1993

Nearly one week later, Loveless called to inform us that he had obtained a partial store list, and he would fax it to us that same day. He further told us that a meeting had been scheduled for Thursday, July 22, at which time the remainder of the stores would be determined and this list would be sent to AMG upon completion. In addition, Loveless stated that he would be giving us lists of advertisers in six-month intervals.

Following his meeting, Loveless called to tell us that he would not be able to fax us a store list, but there would be forty stores in each of five designated states: Oklahoma, Arkansas, Missouri, Texas and Kansas.

He declined to tell us exactly why he would be unable to fax the store list. **It was the one thing we had to have in order to initiate the program.** But, of even greater importance, was the information that was a must for each and every advertiser — where and in how many stores their vendors' ads would be displayed. Any good media and/or marketing person could not possibly make a decision without having this information. But apparently no one at Wal-Mart understood the reasons behind this need, either.

Chapter 11
Do They Know the Meaning of "Best Efforts"?

JULY 29, 1993

It was on this date that our first concrete evidence of Wal-Mart's lack of making any best efforts to sell the program became even more apparent. We received a copy of the memorandum that Loveless sent to the DMM's (divisional merchandise managers), buyers and Wal-Mart's specialty group division.

Attached to each memorandum were copies of all of the materials we had provided to Wal-Mart: results of interviews with Wal-Mart's employees and consumers, our list of advertisers and a color copy of the flyer we had prepared for Wal-Mart to use for selling purposes. This was all well and good. But then the memo further directed the district merchandising managers (DMM's) and all Wal-Mart buyers to solicit and obtain sampling funds **only** in order to support the program. In reality, these funds were nearly non-existent, and certainly a far cry from the national advertising dollars that Wal-Mart was supposed to access. We immediately contacted Loveless to discuss this error, but were told that: "my hands are tied." He had no further comment.

AUGUST 25, 1993

For the past sixty-plus days our offices had been inundated with phone calls from advertisers asking that we provide them information on how to participate in

Wal-Mart's new in-store advertising program. Our response to each of these inquiries was that they needed to contact Wal-Mart.

Immediately thereafter we provided Loveless with the names of the advertisers and asked that he contact them. Needless to say, none were ever contacted by Wal-Mart, to the point that these same advertising representatives called us back to ask why and to seemingly place the blame on our company. Because of this growing frustration — from both us and these potential advertisers — I again called Higham.

He was irate, telling me that "you have no right being involved in the advertising sales, and should get out of it — now." I then apprised him that Matt's memo had directed the buyers to use "sampling funds." This, too, was contrary to all of our direction of the past. Higham's blunt response was that: "I do not have time to read Matt's materials and consequently I am not aware of the program elements. If you need more answers, talk to Matt." He then immediately hung up, giving me no opportunity to respond to his commands.

This conversation made it even more apparent — if possible — that Higham had no intention of allowing the program to be successful. Wal-Mart had not yet, and apparently never did, return a single call to any of the advertisers wishing to participate in the Shoppers Calculator program.

SEPTEMBER 10, 1993

It had now been six weeks since we last spoke with Loveless. Although we had tried countless times and left innumerable messages asking that he return our calls, all went unanswered. Finally on this date, we were successful in reaching him — obviously because he accidentally answered his phone. He told us that the buyers were still selling the advertising, but asked for more time to negotiate advertising contracts. Therefore he was extending the deadline for ad sales to September 22.

On September 21, in advance of the supposed September 22 deadline, we again called Loveless. It, too, was not returned. However, the following day — D-day — we were successful in reaching him. We took this opportunity to again express our concern that he had instructed the buyers to access only "sampling funds." Loveless again expressed his personal frustration by telling us that "his hands remained tied."

Two days later we received a letter from our New York sales consultant, Gene Bay, again asking why he was continuing to receive calls from advertisers wishing to participate, and Wal-Mart was continuing to ignore calls from these same advertisers. He, too, was becoming very frustrated by Wal-Mart's lack of cooperation, and he was operating from a considerable distance.

SEPTEMBER 30, 1993

More than one week after Wal-Mart's stated ad sales deadline, and after having no response to my countless calls to Loveless and/or Higham, as much as I hated to do so, I chose to take my frustration out on each by directing my next letter to Glass.

It was at this time that we first pointed out that Wal-Mart's contractually required best efforts were not being made. In fact they were being wholly ignored. We had provided Wal-Mart with the names of dozens of advertisers wanting to participate in the program, and to our knowledge, they had not followed up with one. I also reminded them of Higham's previous statement to us that "we can sell anything we want to sell, and we certainly don't need anyone's help to do so." It was obvious that someone needed help. Nothing was happening.

Whether it was a result of my letter to Glass, or simply a continuation of Higham's way of dealing with us, we heard no more from anyone, including Glass, Higham or Loveless. No calls were ever returned, nor was there ever any response to any of our numerous attempts at correspondence.

DECEMBER 8, 1993

Then on this date, Cindy Hood, an AMG sales representative, as well as our appointed in-house coordinator for the Wal-Mart program, placed another call to Matt Loveless. To her amazement, he answered his phone. He, too, was astonished, but not so much that we had called, but because he had been told that Higham had contacted us several months previously to inform us of Wal-Mart's decision "not to go forward with the Wal-Mart/Shoppers Calculator program." Again Loveless reiterated that his hands were tied, but he promised to contact Higham and call back with additional information. We never heard from Loveless again. Apparently, in addition to having his "hands tied," he had since been "gagged," too.

After receiving this information from Loveless, I immediately drafted another letter to David Glass. Two days later I received a letter from Paul Higham again telling us that: "the Wal-Mart buyers were not willing to support the program, and consequently, Wal-Mart was not in a position to proceed."

He had used the same "out" we had projected that he would when he previously required insertion of the phrase, "the final decision would be made by the buyers" into the contract.

From that point forward, it had been enormously evident that the buyers would negate the program immediately. First we had been told "they did not want to mess with the program." Next, their buyers were told to access only sampling dollars, a category that was nearly non-existent. And, perhaps best of all, no one from Wal-Mart had ever contacted any of the national advertisers that wanted to participate in the program.

DECEMBER 14, 1993

Wal-Mart had breached its contract by failing to make its "best efforts "to sell the program. In fact, they had made absolutely no efforts to sell the program. I immediately chose to point this out to Higham with copies of my letter to Glass, Fields, and Loveless. My letter emphasized four primary points:

(1) Our company had been misled by Wal-Mart's management for nearly three years.

(2) Paul Higham never had any intention of honoring our contract.

(3) For the past six months, Wal-Mart had made no effort to sell the program.

(4) It was most evident that common courtesy had no place in their manner of conducting business. On the contrary, egos reigned supreme.

Chapter 12

The First Shot Is Fired, but It's off Target!

DECEMBER 28, 1993

On this date, I received a letter of response from Higham. It was obvious that he had re-read the contract and interpreted it in a manner that best suited him. However, in communicating with me he had misquoted and misinterpreted it to the point that rather than being an orderly and business-like communiqué, it read more as a rather frantic attempt to dispute our charges — in any way possible.

Perhaps the most interesting part of his written excuses was the statement that Wal-Mart "did not force" vendors "to participate in any program." Maybe "force" was a bit too powerful a choice of words. But in our case, it had always been "the Higham Way" or the highway. Any Wal-Mart vendor would immediately disagree with this "force" statement. But they would do so only in private, for if such a statement got out, their respective relationships would be history.

Far too many hopeful vendors had been forced out of Wal-Mart — if not out of business — due to their decision or inability not to pay the freight, or participate in one of Wal-Mart's special programs. Their vendors were always played against their competitors. The good news for Wal-Mart was there was always a competitor waiting in the wings, anxious to participate. But, what we did not realize was that within the coming year this technique — the application of force

— would be applied to us, to prevent their vendors from doing business with us, and to "force" us out of business.

Higham's letter pointed out that Wal-Mart had the right to decide whether they wanted to continue the program beyond January 30, 1994. This was December 28, 1993, and it had already been terminated supposedly four months previously. In reality, the date which he should have referenced was June 30, 1994, not January 30, 1994. Such statements in his response made it apparent that it was not just his buyers that "lacked the time or inclination" to "mess with" our program. This disorganized response positioned him at the top of the list.

It was more than evident that Higham had meant what he had said to Gary Young and me previously: this business relationship "could have been much easier" on us had we initially called upon Paul Higham — and no one else. We had truly underestimated the power of Higham's "EGOnomics." In view of that, perhaps the book you're reading should have been re-titled: "*The High-am Mighty.*" His conduct and treatment of us make that title appear to be much more apropos.

Part IV — 1994

Chapter 13

The Power of "EGOnomics!"

JANUARY- FEBRUARY 1994

Shortly after the first of the year, we initiated a search for legal counsel. Not only had Higham breached Wal-Mart's contract with our company, he had done so in an erroneous manner and six months premature of the contract's requirement. It was overtly apparent that Wal-Mart had made absolutely no effort to sell the Shopper's Calculator program, despite being contractually bound to a best-efforts obligation to perform.

I was constantly reminded of Higham's statements to us that: "if you had come to me first, I could have made this a lot easier for you." Wal-Mart's treatment of us for the past six months underscored the importance of our not having initially introduced the program to Higham. We were suffering the results thereof because Higham and/or Wal-Mart did not have any intention of ever using our program.

Disregarding the "ego" factor, their position was increasingly difficult to understand. They knew the results of our more than two and a half years of research, and we had been constantly told of what a wonderful service the calculators provided to both Wal-Mart and their customers.

With the exception of Higham's indifference, we were never informed of any problems — not one. He was saying "no" to a customer service that all but guaranteed to bring Wal-Mart tens of millions of dollars in all new revenues. And perhaps of equal importance, the Wal-Mart customers loved the program — as witnessed by their rating it

8.5-plus on a scale of one to ten. And, this rating was further verified by the one study that Wal-Mart conducted itself. But, as Higham had previously told us: "I could care less what our customers think." **Wal-Mart's "EGOnomics" certainly dominated their sense of "economics."**

On January 25, Jim Sturdivant, of the Tulsa law firm of Gable and Gotwals, sent a letter to Robert K. Rhoads, then general counsel for Wal-Mart Stores, Inc. The letter pointed out that as of this date Wal-Mart had signed two contracts with AMG, and essentially breached each one. Wal-Mart was further advised that it was the hope of AMG that these disputes could be resolved without litigation. However, corrective measures "must happen quickly." Wal-Mart was also put on record to preserve all of its records and information relating to the business relationship. The issues called out referred only to Wal-Mart's contractual obligations. Nothing was mentioned about the methodology employed in dealing with AMG, or any potential tort issues.

Rhonda Parish, a member of Wal-Mart's legal staff, responded by telephone to Jim Sturdivant and David Bryant of Gable and Gotwals on January 31. She agreed to come to Tulsa to meet in Sturdivant's office at 3:00 pm on Friday, February 3. By letter, Sturdivant confirmed the date of the meeting and again reiterated the time and monies that AMG had been losing since August of 1991 — two and a half years previously, when our first test had been initiated. He further stressed the urgency in arriving at an agreement, satisfactory to continuation, by both parties.

At this meeting Ms. Parish's response was that Wal-Mart had been "in the wrong" and they wished to make amends. She asked that Mr. Higham be given an opportunity to meet with AMG in order to determine a satisfactory solution. He apparently recognized the errors that had been committed, and it was his desire to correct them and also avoid legal action.

In accordance with Ms. Parish's promise, Higham called me less than one week later in order to schedule a meeting. We were to meet at 9:00 a.m. on Thursday, February 17, at Wal-Mart. I elected to confirm the meeting by letter and reiterate our concerns, as well as our position.

We had spent the past eighteen months crisscrossing the United States, calling on Wal-Mart's vendors not just to sell the forthcoming program, but to document (for Wal-Mart) the fact that their vendors were anxious to commit dollars from their national advertising budgets to participate in our in-store program.

The overwhelmingly positive results of these calls upon their vendors had been repeatedly given to Wal-Mart. Yet, in his infinite wisdom, Higham had elected to ignore our results and instruct his buyers to sell the program utilizing only sampling dollars.

This meant that the program had been doomed from the start, and it was my position that the only way to get it kick-started was for ADDvantage Media to be the only seller, selling it to the managers of the national ad budgets of Wal-Mart's vendors. But, regardless, whatever the solution was to be, it was imperative that Wal-Mart support it — and do so in a vigorous, believable manner.

Chapter 14

It's a New Beginning, and Matt Is Nowhere to Be Seen.

FEBRUARY 17, 1994

Although our legal counsel did not accompany us, Gary Young and I met with Paul Higham, Rhonda Parish, Barbara Brown and Maureen Gustafson, the latter having been selected to be our future liaison. Matt Lovelace was conspicuous by his absence.

An obviously irritated Higham set the meeting's tone immediately, telling us that his buyers "did not want to mess with the program." Although we had heard this too many times previously, it was in enormous contrast to the messages given to us from the outset by Loveless. He had continually assured us that the advertising was being successfully sold and the buyers were having "no difficulty" selling it. And, we believed Matt because this was an "overlay" of our selling experiences.

Our response to Higham was to again tell him all of the reasons that we should be allowed to sell the program. We stressed that we would not be contacting any of their existing revenue sources. We would only be calling upon the national ad budgets of Wal-Mart's vendors. We expressed and documented the excitement of their vendors, knowing they would soon be able to participate in a Wal-Mart in-store program. But if we were to be successful in selling the program, it was imperative that we install our calculators in enough stores to command the attention of these same advertisers.

Their proposed program, consisting of a total of 200 stores, with forty stores being spread out in each of five separate states, had no appeal. It lacked critical mass. Also, we preferred not to have to service the calculators in minimal number of stores in a wide-spread area (five states).

We requested that Wal-Mart designate one of their leading sales regions with a store count of well in excess of two hundred stores. We further agreed that the 230-store Texas region, which had three "top-ten" marketplaces, would offer sufficient "sizzle" to gain the attention of the advertisers. We also emphasized that we would need more Wal-Mart cooperation than had been given us in the past.

We were then told that Wal-Mart would provide us with all of the materials we had previously requested, and needed, to sell the program. We were asked to prepare a new contract that would shift the selling responsibility to AMG, as opposed to Wal-Mart personnel. **We had sought each of these stipulations for the past two and a half years.**

Prior to the end of this meeting, it was clearly stated that time was of the essence. The peak selling time had already expired — those months immediately preceding the start of the calendar year, when advertisers traditionally prepare their annual budgets and advertising allocations — and it would be difficult to convince advertisers to change their commitments.

We left the meeting targeting March 15 as the date to have a contract in place and for us to be in possession of all of the necessary marketing data. We were to have the store list well in advance of that time. It was our further hope that by having a contract by the middle of March, we might have the opportunity to capture a portion of the '94 advertising budgets, at least a part of those not yet expended. In view of the importance of a Wal-Mart program, we were optimistic about being able to shift them from some of the other media they had previously planned to use.

Chapter 15

The Players Change, but Our Treatment Remains the Same.

MARCH, APRIL, MAY 1994

What had been promised and projected to be no more than a three-week turn-around for a signed contract, store location lists, all necessary marketing data, etc. — predictably turned into the same Wal-Mart runaround.

Three weeks after the conclusion of our meeting with Higham, Gustafson advised us that she was sending the store locations list. We received it one week later.

On March 15, we again requested a signed contract, and further store-marketing information. From March 15 through May 31, despite our innumerable phone calls and messages, we received no response from anyone. It was obvious that even our newest contact, Maureen, had been pre-instructed on how to communicate with us — **DON'T**.

Again, in view of their lack of response, I contacted Jim Sturdivant at our Tulsa legal firm and provided him with a draft of a letter that I proposed be sent to Higham. The message was that more than one hundred days had lapsed since our last meeting. Sturdivant agreed, and immediately sent Parish this message.

Apparently, legal contact was the only type of communication they understood, as again it worked. One week later a signed contract was returned to our offices.

Obviously, we had waited too long to have our attorneys again act on our behalf. Unfortunately "legalese" appeared to be the only language Wal-Mart understood.

JUNE, JULY 1994

Having finally secured the revised and signed contract, we contacted Dave Lienemann at Wal-Mart's Supercenters and pointed out that his program had now been suspended for two years, awaiting the results of the "final" in-store test. This "sixty-day" test had been successfully completed, and it was now time for reinstatement of our Supercenter/Hypermart program in accordance with their commitment of two years ago. Then at the direction of Maureen Gustafson, we drafted a "joint" news release and sent it to John Hamilton for approval.

On June 23, more than four months after our Wal-Mart meeting establishing the parameters of a new contract, we had a follow-up meeting with Wal-Mart. This time it was with Maureen Gustafson. Matt Loveless had mysteriously disappeared and was never to be heard from again — at least by us. We were later told that he had been transferred out of the marketing department. My guess was that his departure was directly related to our relationship with him and the manner in which he handled it. He had seen the benefits of the program and probably had expounded thereon. But any reported success was in violation of Higham's plans for us and the Shopper's Calculator program. Consequently, my further guess was that because of his obvious cooperation and encouragement of us, he had been sent off to "Siberia" at Higham's direction — away from his regime. But this was purely speculation on my part, for no one was willing to discuss Loveless at any time thereafter.

At this meeting with Gustafson, our news releases were approved and returned to us for release to the trade and consumer publications. But we found ourselves at square one again relative to being given any of the store sales and traffic data. Fortunately, we had prepared a sales folder that we were able to leave with Maureen for her to fill in the blanks and answer our specific questions.

The very next day Maureen responded, giving us their specific changes to the folder. These alterations were made and again we appeared to be off and running.

Gustafson initially proved to be very responsible and helpful in obtaining the information that we needed. She provided us with the majority of the requested information and actually sent letters to the Wal-Mart store managers alerting them to the forthcoming installations of Shopper's Calculators in their respective stores.

Following up on our receipt of the newly signed contract, I contacted Dave Lieneman regarding the continuation of our Supercenter/Hypermart program. We had hoped to include it under the same terms we had agreed upon with Wal-Mart. Lienemann had previously told us that if and when Wal-Mart did approve the test, the Supercenters/Hypermarts would then reinstate the contract under the same terms to which Wal-Mart had agreed. Although this test had taken two years as opposed to the two months that had been specified, it was now time for this reinstatement.

However, Lienemann again had a new boss and told us that we would need to speak to Bobby Bland, his new supervisor. After several unsuccessful attempts to reach Bobby Bland, I discovered that he was no longer with the company, and had not been for several weeks. Upon discussing this further with Dave Lienemann, I was told that John Hamilton had replaced Bland and Bland would be my future contact. We needed a program to keep up with the cast. Nonetheless, I contacted Hamilton on July 25.

Wal-Mart had approved our advertiser's brochure and our proposed program-announcement letters to their vendors, and both were finally ready to go to print. Simultaneously, we began hiring more sales representatives and also updated our lists of customer profiles, their average number of visits per week, etc. Gustafson's standard response seemed only to be "I don't believe we have those statistics, but I will look into it." The good thing was that Gustafson apparently had the ear of Higham, whereas Loveless had appeared to receive only lip service from him, if and when he received any response at all.

AUGUST, SEPTEMBER 1994

I continued to attempt to reach John Hamilton in hopes of obtaining a decision to include the Wal-Mart Supercenters and Hypermarts in an all-inclusive Wal-Mart program. This would provide us with more stores and more customers and justify a higher rate per cycle to the advertisers.

It had now been nearly ninety days since I had initially re-contacted Lienemann in order to obtain an answer, and it had been more than six weeks since I had last contacted Hamilton. My follow-up phone calls and messages continued to go unanswered. Hamilton was obviously consistent with what now appeared to be a corporate dictate — never return our phone calls. They obviously had the feeling that to do so would be disruptive to their daily workloads.

We had several advertisers that wanted to commence immediately, but we were reluctant to initiate any twelve-month contracts with just a few advertisers. We were hopeful of being able to start with a full slate of advertisers (ten) in order to maximize the return to both Wal-Mart and ourselves.

In early September, I contacted Higham to ask about the potential of extending the contract to eighteen months. This extra six months would allow us to get "up to speed" prior to the start of the existing twelve-month agreement. And, there would be a far greater revenue return to Wal-Mart upon which we hoped to be judged for the future.

To my surprise, Higham agreed to the extension of our contract from twelve months to eighteen months, but at the same time he instructed John Hamilton to cancel the Supercenter agreement. These actions were contradictory and again made absolutely no sense to us. But they were consistent with Higham's past actions; and they apparently made sense to him, because just two weeks after my request for the six-month extension, an addendum to our contract was returned to us for signature. One week later, a copy signed by Higham, was also returned.

Finally we were of the belief that we were actually going to initiate and sell a Wal-Mart in-store advertising program – in at least a 200-store network. Because of this belief, we launched an all-out effort to retain some of America's best sales consultants and manufacturers' representatives to sell our program. My initial efforts were focused on some of the very best sales people I had met and worked with during my career in the advertising agency business.

Some of these sales people were still active and others had semi-retired to become sales consultants. Two of those in the consultant category were Gene Bay and Larre Barrett. Both were all-stars in the media-selling business. Gene had previously enjoyed a very successful career with *CBS* before becoming publisher of *Field and Stream* magazine. When the magazine was sold, Gene went on to become a nearly full-time consultant for *ESPN*. But, because he was so excited about the potential of our program, he

consented to "squeeze" us into his tight schedule and func-
tion as our East Coast sales consultant.

Larre Barrett had previously headed the sales staffs
for *ABC Sports* and later headed the Olympics sales staff
for *CBS.* Having just wrapped up his Olympics sales job for
CBS, and believing that a Wal-Mart in-store media would be
very appealing to his clients, Larre also agreed to become
one of our sales consultants.

We then added several of America's leading media
rep groups, rounding out what I believed to be the absolute
best sales group available. In all cases, this entire group
was confident that our program would be a very appealing
media buy for their entire client base. And, I was of the opinion that if this group could not sell the Wal-Mart program,
absolutely no one could. They were all extremely talented
sales people, and all were headquartered in the major cities
where the major advertisers were located.

Chapter 16

The Advertisers Ask Questions and Wal-Mart Gives the Wrong Answers.

One of our representatives in the Atlanta area conducted some due diligence to determine the potential of the Wal-Mart program with his current advertising client list. One of the first people he talked to was Meg Carlton at the Russell Corporation (Jerzees clothing) who told him that our program would have no appeal to her. She further told him that Wal-Mart had previously advised her that they wanted Jerzees to participate solely in Wal-Mart programs, not programs offered for sale by outside vendors.

This was our first indication of the stigma that Wal-Mart had already placed upon advertising programs conducted by anyone other than themselves. This response struck us as unbelievable. After all, Wal-Mart had engaged us to sell their **only** in-store program, and they had just extended the contract from twelve to eighteen months. This time they had to be sincere, right?

OCTOBER 1994

Only a few days later, we were notified by a letter from Procter & Gamble that "after careful review, we have determined that it is in our best interest ...that you (AD-Dvantage Media) no longer be one of our approved Core Suppliers." This letter followed recommendations from five of the P&G ad agencies that at least five of their brands participate in the program. These proponents had described our program as being one of the "highest-impact ad programs available to these products."

Obviously the Wal-Mart buyers had wasted no time in alerting P&G not to do business with us. And, P&G, in order to avoid any potential criticism from Wal-Mart, had expedited its communication with us, making certain that we no longer "tempted" any of their advertising or marketing personnel with an opportunity to participate in our Wal-Mart program.

Here was a company that not only was one of America's largest single advertisers, but did a very high percentage of its total corporate volume with Wal-Mart. Also, P&G had previously advertised on our Shopper's Calculators in our grocery store network, for products including Tide, Pringles, Citrus Hill Orange Juice, Oxydol, Hawaiian Punch, Folgers, Dash, Jif, Puffs, Bounty, Pampers, Downy and White Cloud. The research conducted to evaluate the movement of each of these products confirmed sales increases of no less than double digits — in each and every case.

How could a company that had previously granted us vendor approval, had used our calculators to promote more than a dozen of their corporate products — and gained huge increases in the sale of each — now ignore an opportunity to promote its products within the aisles of the Wal-Mart stores? Not only was their action incredible, it was truly non-sensible. I contacted L. Ross Love, vice president of advertising for the Procter & Gamble Company, to tell him just that. Needless to say, my letters and phone calls to Mr. Love received no response.

On the very same day that Procter & Gamble refused to recognize us as a future vendor, Heinz Pet Foods had a similar message for us. They did not wish to participate in our program because their past experience with such programs always ended with Wal-Mart buyers asking them not to participate.

Wal-Mart's explanation to Heinz was that they would rather have them give (Wal-Mart's buyers) the money to reduce the price of their merchandise or to participate in other "Wal-Mart programs."

It was rapidly becoming apparent that we had been enlisted to scout for and turn up new monies — not for our Shopper's Calculator program, but for the availability of new sources of the special promotional funds constantly sought by Wal-Mart's buyers.

Within this same time frame our Wal-Mart contact, Maureen Gustafson, left on maternity leave. Shortly thereafter we discovered that Wal-Mart had no intention of appointing someone to replace her — again a contract violation. We were only told that she would return to work late in November. She never did, and it was not until we again threatened to file suit that Wal-Mart notified us that they were appointing someone else to work with us and serve as the program coordinator. **But, who and when?**

Despite the commitment to provide us with an internal coordinator, it did not happen. This was a critical time and they had again put us out on a limb. In the midst of having numerous advertisers ready to participate in the program, there was no one within Wal-Mart that they could contact to further discuss the program.

Our first real need for this representative was with Cadbury Beverages. Cadbury's national advertising personnel found the program to have exciting potential. As a necessary follow-up, they had asked their national accounts director, Chuck Ginski, to discuss the merits of the

Shopper's Calculator program with Wal-Mart. In following up with his Wal-Mart buyer, Brent Hardin, Ginski was told that he (Hardin) knew nothing about the program. Ginski then called us to say that we needed to have a Wal-Mart representative apprise Hardin of the program and its merits, and basically to verify that the program was alive and well, and was one that would benefit both the advertisers and Wal-Mart. In other words, they needed approval from Wal-Mart before they could participate.

I placed several unsuccessful phone calls to Paul Higham. I also contacted him by letter stating that "any word of encouragement and explanation of the program would be beneficial to all concerned." I further advised him that the popular response from buyers was: "the program doesn't work," or "I don't know anything about the program," or "rather than do that program why not give us the money directly, instead." Higham kept with his well-established habits. I received no response, by phone or letter.

NOVEMBER 1994

This was a very revealing and eventful month. First, Chuck Ginski, with Cadbury Beverages, again contacted us to express his frustration with his Wal-Mart buyers and their accompanying lack of knowledge and enthusiasm for the program.

Cadbury had been ready to commit to the program two months prior in order to participate in the November and December ad cycles. However, at that time his buyer told him to "wait and look at the program for the coming year." At the end of October, Ginski again met with his Wal-Mart buyer, who this time told him simply not to participate. He gave no further reasons. Being a concerned vendor, Ginski was certainly not in a position to commit to the program until his buyer endorsed it. He continued to be unable to understand why this buyer had also told him that he was unfamiliar with the Shopper's Calculator program. Such statements from Wal-Mart's buyers again made it most apparent that they had never been advised of the program, even during Wal-Mart's first attempt to sell it — via the buyers — and probably not even yet. Had they been given any type of information on the program, they certainly would have been "aware" of it, and now they were supposed to be endorsing it to assist AMG's selling efforts. Again, this was more evidence of Wal-Mart's previous "no efforts" to sell our program, as opposed to their contractually required "best efforts."

On this very same day, Gene Bay, our New York sales consultant, contacted us again to say that he had been a part of many, many very positive meetings with companies in New York; however, "the enthusiasm seems to dwindle once these companies contact Wal-Mart." Bay asked that we continue to follow-up with Wal-Mart to determine why there was a negative reaction from what seemed to be all of Wal-Mart's buyers and other personnel. He urged us to turn it into a positive for the future.

Our initial contact with the Pepsi Cola Company was with Brian Swete, vice president of marketing in Somers, New York. He passed the media packet along to Mark Simon, Pepsi's Dallas representative, who contacted us at Swete's request. On November 1, Simon, too, expressed strong interest in the program and said that he naturally needed to discuss it further with Wal-Mart before committing. His buyer was also Brent Hardin.

When Simon brought up the subject of the program, Hardin's immediate response to him was that "Wal-Mart had tried the program, knew that *'it did not work,'* and he did not want Pepsi participating in the program."

Understandably, Simon apprised AMG that without Wal-Mart's approval and blessing, he would not be able to

123

participate in the program. He further requested that we determine why Wal-Mart was not endorsing the program and to contact him once we had an answer. He expressed his continued interest in participating as an advertiser, but he could not do so as long as Wal-Mart said "no."

Unfortunately, these negative responses were not confined to Wal-Mart's beverage buyers. They appeared to be across the board. When Bob Vogle, Block Drug Company, advised his Wal-Mart buyers that his company planned to support the movement of their products by participating in this in-store program, he too was told not to participate. Instead, "they should give the monies directly to Wal-Mart" in order to participate in some of Wal-Mart's other promotional programs.

This same week we also called and wrote to Wal-Mart again, requesting that they provide us with a person to contact, and one with whom our advertisers could visit and discuss the merits of our program. Again, we received no response to our request.

Cindy Cox spoke with Jim Marsteller at Ralston-Purina. He was enthused over the prospects of the program. Not only could they use it to promote their own brands of dog foods, but he felt it would be good to use to promote Wal-Mart's private label dog food – a brand that accounted for a large percentage of his company's dog food production.

On this same date, Gene Bay called to further express his concern for his apparent inability to sell the Wal-Mart program. As he stated, "I am beginning to wonder what's going on at Wal-Mart. All I hear is 'I have to check with my Wal-Mart person' — and nothing positive comes back." Gene concluded our conversation by asking, "What do we need to do to get Wal-Mart to endorse or be enthusiastic about our program?"

In a period of one week, Wal-Mart representatives had told at least six of their vendors — and our advertising prospects — not to participate in the Shopper's Calculator program. At the end of this same week I penned a letter for our attorneys to send on their letterhead to Wal-Mart's legal department. It was more than clear that something needed to happen, and it needed to happen now.

But it was the recommendation of our legal counsel that they not send another letter, but instead contact Rhonda Parish by phone. Granted, I had vented my spleen and it was perhaps inappropriate to do so at that time. However, I deemed it to be appropriate because if Wal-Mart were not forced to cease their negative responses to advertisers immediately, our program and our company would soon be history.

On November 11, Gable & Gotwals again contacted Rhonda Parish, and three days later, we were told that Wal-Mart would soon be appointing another employee to work with us on our program. They just needed to get this new appointee up to speed. Shortly thereafter, our legal counsel again contacted Ms. Parish, this time giving her the names of six of the prospective advertisers who had been told directly or indirectly not to participate in the Shopper's Calculator program.

During this same time, we were contacted by Anni Gibson of the Procter and Gamble Company. Mr. Love had been thoughtful enough to ask that she contact us to explain why we were being denied the further opportunity to sell the Wal-Mart program to P&G, and perhaps of greater importance, why P&G had elected to revoke our status of being an "approved vendor." The answer to each question was the same. As she explained to me, our association with Wal-Mart "created certain difficulties." She refused to further elaborate. My response was that it was extremely difficult for me to understand how our vendor status could be re-voked within five days of our introduction of the Wal-Mart program to their media and advertising departments. She had no explanation, but it was again more than apparent that Wal-Mart had given P&G the same message as they had given to every other vendor that was considering par-ticipation in the Shopper's Calculator program: "The Shop-per's Calculator program doesn't work. Give us the money instead!"

What Wal-Mart's management obviously did not re-alize — or care about — was that by causing us to lose our "approved vendor" status with P&G, they cost us entry into the doors of America's largest single advertiser. This action negated all future sales to P&G for not just the Wal-Mart pro-gram, but it would have a huge impact upon the programs presently in Kmart and potentially any and all of the other mass merchandisers presently considering the installation of our program. This list also included numerous grocery chains, as well as Home Depot, Lowe's, and many others.

This was another of Wal-Mart's odious actions that was taken wholly without any forethought as to the damage it could cause. But, in retrospect — and what is even more chilling — maybe they knew exactly what they were doing to us. Whichever way it was, it prob-ably cost AMG hundreds of thousands of dollars, if not millions, in future lost sales. But so what? Wal-Mart's ego-driven greed continued to appear as if it had no monetary limits, nor did they have any concerns, what-soever, for our future.

Chapter 17

They Say They're Only "Rolling Back Prices" but They Are "Rolling Over" Us.

DECEMBER 1994

Rhonda Parish responded to our legal counsel's correspondence, this time advising them that "Paul Higham and Wal-Mart had no interest in meeting with anyone from our company in order to correct or to compensate AMG for the harm resulting from Wal-Mart's handling of the program to date."

After some discussion, and being aware that an irreparable relationship with Wal-Mart would only hurt us and serve no productive purpose, we elected to request that Wal-Mart simply take three remedial actions: (1) immediately issue an internal memo to Wal-Mart buyers (the content of which we would provide) endorsing the program; (2) immediately mail a supportive letter to the advertisers who had been alienated to date; and (3) have a Wal-Mart representative make phone calls to each of these memo recipients to encourage them to participate in the Wal-Mart/Shopper's Calculator program. This message was sent to Ms. Parish, and we anxiously awaited the response.

In the meantime, Dean Zeko, our Dallas-based sales consultant, called to say that he "felt something strange was going on with regard to the Wal-Mart/Shopper's Calculator program." He continued to say that "our rep group has made too many calls where the potential advertiser was initially very excited about the opportunity offered by our program. However, within time, their enthusiasm declined dramatically. What's the problem?"

Less than a week later, our sales consultant, Dan Kellner, wrote us to recap his 1994 selling experiences relative to the Wal-Mart program. As he stated, "With the last days of 1994 drawing to a close, I thought it would be apropos to look at the successes we have enjoyed over the past months." He further said, "Unfortunately the monetary gains we all anticipated from this program have not come through. I really do not have an answer to the 'why'" of this question, but I think we should review some of the accounts." He proceeded to point out that 7-UP, after being very excited about the program and knowing they only needed to sell ten cases per day, per store, to pay for the entire program, later told him they could not participate "due to the cost of the program." The media person on the same account was "stunned" by this reasoning. She had run the numbers and determined that it was a great media value and a great promotional vehicle to support the sales of 7-UP in all of the Wal-Mart stores.

Kellner further pointed out that Pennzoil, whose sales through Wal-Mart were a significant part of their total volume, was very high on the proposal from the outset. It had been later related to Kellner that the agency presented it to Pennzoil, and even the Pennzoil national accounts manager — in charge of the Wal-Mart account — had loved the program. Two months later Kellner was told by the agency that the program was "dead," and no further explanation was offered.

As he further stated, "I bring this up because something very strange is happening here. We've had innumerable very positive feedbacks from both clients and their agencies in regard to the Shopper's Calculator program. Then in all cases they decline to participate, with no further comment. It is almost as if they are 'afraid to be a participant.' Things always look great, then they decline, and nobody can explain the 'why' of their negative decision."

He additionally pointed out that his experience had been that the program has "always been very well-received. However, it always seems to die when it gets to the level of the account person in charge of servicing and selling Wal-Mart."

Although we had not yet discussed with our regional sales representatives any of the Wal-Mart buyer difficulties we had discovered, we continued to get precisely the same feedback from each of them. This made it even more apparent that the "poisoning" of the minds of our advertising prospects was far more widespread than we had thought. Our initial thought was that simply one or two buyers had been "bad-mouthing and negating" the program. But now it was very apparent that it was widespread — across the board — with all Wal-Mart buyers and merchandising personnel.

Five days after requesting Wal-Mart's assistance in correcting the problems their buyers had created, we received Wal-Mart's response:

(1)   They were willing to distribute a memo to buyers; however, the memo would not endorse the program nor would it encourage the buyers to support the program. Instead, it would simply state that Wal-Mart had a contract with ADDvantage Media Group, Inc. for an in-store advertising program;

(2)   They would not send a letter to potential advertisers, nor would they make any follow-up calls on our behalf to any of our potential advertisers.

The bottom line was that they refused to do anything to cooperate, perhaps in a very awkward attempt not to admit the guilt that their people's actions had placed upon them to date. As related to us by Ms. Parish, this had been yet another Higham decision.

Shortly thereafter, Kimberly-Clark took a different approach to backing out of our program. After telling us for more than three months that they planned to participate, using our packaged-goods concept (in their case, a calculator produced as a replica of a Kleenex box), they simply failed to return phone calls. Finally, when reached, they continued to say they liked the program, but found themselves unable to authorize use of it until they received an approval from their personnel in charge of the Wal-Mart account. In this case, each of our meetings with Kimberly-Clark had been with the vice president of advertising, who apparently never did hear anything positive from his "Wal-Mart people."

By mid-December Gene Bay was again calling us to relate his concerns about the "Wal-Mart situation." He told us that he "continued to believe that potential advertisers accepted" his presentations of the program on "very high notes," but they seemingly always lost interest once they talked to their Wal-Mart personnel. As he further stated, "Until we figure out why, I would be wasting my time by continuing to make sales calls on AMG's behalf."

This same week our Michigan sales representatives contacted us to say that the Andrew Jergens Company, after planning to utilize the program, called to say that they would be unable to do so. The reason given was that their Wal-Mart buyers did not want them to participate in the Shopper's Calculator program. In this case, their Wal-Mart buyer told them that they Andrew Jergens "would be much better off" if they gave Wal-Mart their promotional dollars, as opposed to supporting their products with the ads on the calculators. The representative went further to say, "I wonder if Wal-Mart knows that its buyers are shooting this program down?"

It was further related that the Andrew Jergens marketing department was declining at the request of their executive director of sales for Wal-Mart. Both Wal-Mart's cosmetics and soap buyers had recommended to the Andrew Jergens marketing personnel that they not participate in the calculator program.

The aforementioned reports from our sales personnel, in combination with Wal-Mart's very indignant response to our difficulties, prompted us to seek further counsel from Jim Sturdivant and David Bryant, of our Tulsa-based law firm of Gable and Gotwals. We needed their endorsement of what we believed to be the only solution to our Wal-Mart difficulties — litigation.

Although we thoroughly discussed the numerous pros and cons associated with any litigation, we found the major deterrent to be the monetary power and the size of the stick wielded by the "world's largest retailer" — especially in its home state, where the trial would have to be conducted. However, we all believed in the strength of our case, and because of the strength of our belief, we immediately began our search for Arkansas-based legal counsel. We needed outstanding Arkansas litigators who would not be intimidated by Wal-Mart's gorilla-like presence and behavior, since our contract stipulated that any complaint must be filed in the state of Arkansas.

At this point we again sought the counsel of Bill Atherton, the Tulsa businessman and board member who had previously introduced me to David Glass. He in turn contacted some of Arkansas's leading businessmen and corporate attorneys on our behalf. The CEO of one of Arkansas's largest and most successful companies had gone so far as to tell us that "there is only one person capable of going up against Wal-Mart, and doing so successfully. Our attorneys have had occasion to 'do battle' with him on several occasions, and the SOB defeated us each time." And, he was not alone. Among the majority of the business leaders we contacted, Tom Mars had the reputation of being "young, brilliant and virtually fearless." It was this general consensus that led me to call Tom Mars, a partner in the Fayetteville firm of Everett, Mars & Stills. After a rather lengthy verbal explanation of our "predicament," the following letter was sent to Mars — further outlining our situation in detail and confirming our meeting for 9:00 a.m. on January 3, 1995.

ADDvantage Media Group, Inc.

Shoppers Calculator™

CHARLES H. HOOD
President

December 15, 1994

Mr. Thomas Mars
Everett, Mars & Stills
3822 North Parkview
Fayetteville, AR 72703

Dear Tom,

As a follow up to our conversation, I've enclosed what I believe to be the majority of materials necessary to quickly get you up to speed on our company, our product and our three and one-half years of time and monies invested in Wal-Mart. Our product, the Shoppers Calculator is included. What is not included are the stainless steel screws, brackets and clamps necessary to attach this unit to the handle of a shopping cart. To better see what these units look like on shopping carts, I would suggest that you visit the Bentonville Wal-Mart store. Although no ads are yet in place, you will notice Wal-Mart messages similar to that on the enclosed unit.

I've enclosed my entire file gathered over three and one-half years of dealings with various people at Wal-Mart. I've also prepared a sequential calendar scenario which records events and data as they occurred. In addition you will find a Wal-Mart sales kit, as well as my memo to David Bryant (Gable & Gotwals) outlining damages as I see them. One item in the sales kit which you may want to note would be our advertiser rate card. If we were to sell the entire program for the 18-months of the current contract, this translates into a potential revenue of $12 million. Finally, I've also enclosed other materials relating to our company and our Wal-Mart program.

Tom, our company is approximately five years old. We originally installed our Shoppers Calculators in grocery store chains where we were one of many in-store media companies competing for the projected one hundred billion dollars available for product promotion in the in-store advertising category. We had achieved a media network size of approximately 1,500 grocery stores at the time we obtained our first Wal-Mart contract. Based upon the very positive results of research conducted by both Wal-Mart and ourselves, the positive comments made by Wal-Mart management and the apparent opportunity to be <u>the only</u> in-store media in all Wal-Mart stores, we redirected our entire marketing thrust. We deinstalled all grocery stores, reassigned our entire sales staff to selling a Wal-Mart program and virtually went from the grocery store industry to the mass merchant industry overnight. The bottom line was "why sell advertising in Harvest Foods when you can be selling it for Wal-Mart".

In reviewing the file you will notice that as of June 1992, a contract had been drawn up (and finalized by Wal-Mart's legal department) for the installation of our Shoppers Calculators in <u>all</u> Wal-Mart stores. Unfortunately, on the day before the scheduled signing, Paul Higham, Vice President of Advertising for Wal-Mart, entered the picture and canceled the agreement. At that time he specifically stated to both me and Frank Jerd (AMG VP Sales) that had we introduced the program through him we would not have had any difficultly. Unfortunately, David Glass had been our "guide" and Mr. Higham's name was never mentioned. And, as you may know, Wal-Mart doesn't exactly give you a road map of their executive offices and certainly not the names and titles of their management.

Although the contract was not signed at this time, Mr. Higham did agree to a final 90-day test in the Bentonville Supercenter. His stated intention was to conduct more research and determine whether or not the calculator program could actually be beneficial to him and his department. That 90-day test turned into a 6-month period of time, at the end of which — despite extremely positive research — Paul Higham apprised us that he did not want the program because he did not want us involved in his advertising. At that point, we were able to convince him to allow us to call upon advertisers and document to him that his vendors were willing to spend dollars from their national advertising budgets (as opposed to the sales slush funds which Wal-Mart was already accessing). This would allow Wal-Mart to obtain an <u>all new source of revenue</u>. For the next year our entire sales force validated the fact that dollars could be obtained from the national advertising budgets of all of Wal-Mart's vendors. The level of excitement for the potential of the opportunity to participate in a Wal-Mart in-store program was outstanding. Upon presentation of this evidence to Higham, he agreed to what was signed contract number two. However, he elected to switch the ad sales responsibility from us to Wal-Mart. This contract called for Wal-Mart to make their "best efforts" in the sale of the advertising.

For the next seven months we were contacted by national advertisers interested in the Wal-Mart/Shoppers Calculator program. We forwarded their messages, but Wal-Mart made no effort to contact any of them. When we contacted Wal-Mart about their lack of "follow-up" we were told they no longer wanted to do the program. The reasons given us were two-fold, either their buyers "did not want to mess with the program", or "were unable to sell the program." In reality, no one had even attempted to sell the program. But it would have been difficult since they never did actually specify which of their stores would be participating. Obviously their interpretation of "best efforts" was "no efforts."

When it was called to their attention that they had actually breached this contract, they elected to give us a new contract, the terms of which would be a specified 220 stores and we would sell the advertising. We accepted these terms despite knowing the difficulties of selling a limited regional program. But it was an opportunity to continue to prove to Wal-Mart the value of the Shoppers Calculator program.

After the signing of this contract we produced literature and virtually turned loose 13 sales people to call on all of the advertisers whom we had previously established as having a legitimate interest in a Wal-Mart/Shoppers Calculator program. Again, the opportunity for vendors to promote their products by way of the only in-store advertising program in Wal-Mart was extremely well received. After all, approximately 30% of the total sales of all of Wal-Mart's major vendors are through Wal-Mart outlets. Consequently, it was not a "difficult sell", especially since advertisers could obtain category exclusivity and display their ads in Wal-Mart at the time when up to 80% of all buying decisions are made. Furthermore, the program was priced to advertisers at a highly competitive cost per thousand, a cpm that was less than any other media available (television, newspaper, radio, billboard, etc.).

From the very beginning the advertiser responses to the program were extremely positive. Then in October of this year the advertisers (who had previously intended to purchase schedules in the Wal-Mart program) began to call us and tell our sales people that they were not going to participate. They had told their Wal-Mart buyers that they intended to support the sale of their product with the Shoppers Calculator program, and Wal-Mart told them "don't do it", "it doesn't work", etc.

To this day, I believe that the advertisers who actually advised us of Wal-Mart's posture, represent only the "tip of the iceberg". Without exception our sales personnel have all said: "I've never made a sales presentation that was so well received (to the extent that advertisers said they would definitely want to participate at the time of the initial call.) However, the natural course of action was to tell Wal-Mart what they were going to do. Then in all cases, after advising Wal-Mart, the potential advertisers either quit returning our phone calls, or simply said they were no longer interested in the program."

As stated on the phone, I believe a classic example of the Wal-Mart influence was Procter and Gamble's notification to us that we were no longer considered a vendor. Prior to calling on P&G to sell the Wal-Mart program, they had spent several hundred thousand dollars with us — in our grocery store programs. But, within a few weeks of alerting P&G to our Wal-Mart program, our approved vendor status was canceled. This was done despite the fact that we were "the only game in town", ours being the only in-store opportunity in America's #1 retailer.

In the future without Wal-Mart's assistance — their having poisoned the program — we will never be able to sell our program. We've lost the potential of $12 million revenue for the 200 store program and potentially ten times that much for a national program. We've also lost all of the dollars ($1.5 to $2.0 million) which we elected to invest to prove to Wal-Mart that the program had great merit.

Today, we are also on the threshold of obtaining a contract for a program in Kmart. Wal-Mart's statements to advertisers that "we tried the program and it doesn't work" could even place this program in the "terminal" category, resulting in ever greater damage to the future of our company.

I do not believe that our program was killed in a malicious manner. I believe it stemmed from the left-hand not knowing what the right-hand was doing. Paul Higham never did live up to his contractual obligations. He never did advise the buyers of the program nor the contractual obligations of Wal-Mart. Because the buyers were never notified of the program their actions were dictated by human nature. All of a sudden they were presented with vendors coming to them to tell them they intended to spend hundreds of thousands of dollars on a Wal-Mart in-store advertising program. Because these same buyers are compensated based upon sales volume of the goods which they purchase and dollars they are able to squeeze from these same vendors (promotional slush funds), they saw this as a huge opportunity to redirect these all new sources of revenue into their own department coffers. By essentially seizing these funds they simultaneously killed the Shoppers Calculator program and very possibly our entire company.

I trust that this overview, plus the files enclosed will enable you to get up to speed in advance of our 9:00 a.m. meeting on January 3. As stated, Craig Hoster, Baker & Hoster, my brother in-law and one of our six initial investors will accompany me at that time. Craig has lived this entire scenario in a somewhat vicarious manner. He also has studied the entire file and has certain legal views to discuss.

Thank you again for agreeing to meet with us.

Cordially,

CHH:se

enclosures:

cc: Craig Hoster
    Bill Atherton

Part V — 1995

Chapter 18

We Take a "Trip to Mars!"

JANUARY 3, 1995

It was on this date that Gary Young and I drove to Fayetteville for our initial meeting with Tom Mars and his associates. We took with us a comprehensive seven-page outline that documented each of our meetings, phone calls and correspondence with Wal-Mart personnel — that had occurred between June of '91 (when we initially met with David Glass) through this date, January 3, 1995.

We informed Tom that this outline was supported by more than eleven thousand pages of documentation. This documentation included the many call reports — copies of which were always mailed to Wal-Mart in order to confirm the decisions made in each meeting — that recorded the content of each meeting and the decisions made therein. By doing so, we ascertained that all Wal-Mart personnel — present in the meeting or on the call — concurred with our resulting interpretations. This documentation further contained copies of ALL correspondence between our Wal-Mart contacts and our company's management team.

Much to our surprise, Tom was even more youthful than we had expected. He was neatly and casually attired in sharply creased Levis and a dress shirt. But from the outset, his casual attire belied his thorough and extremely professional approach. After attentively listening to our perhaps too-repetitious verbal descriptions and overviews of our Wal-Mart situation, he consented to further study our materials in advance of making his final decision about representing us, and how he felt it best to proceed. Before we left his office, he asked that we bring copies of all eleven thousand pages of our support documents when we returned for our next meeting.

Although we were very excited about the potential of Mars representing us, I dreaded having to tell our office manager (and my long-time administrative assistant), Sue Estep, of the need for all of this data to be copied and packaged for review by our attorneys. But it was a necessity, and if anyone was well enough organized to accomplish this, it was Sue. True to form, within a very few days, Sue had it copied, packaged, and ready for us to take back to Fayetteville.

Note: The following are copies of the seven-page, abbreviated "scenario" delivered to Tom Mars at the time of our initial visit:

Walmart's EGONOMICS

Wal-Mart Scenario —
Shoppers Calculators

6-91	Bill Atherton and Chuck Hood call on David Glass
7-91	Chuck Hood meets with Dave Lienemann
9-91	Contract signed for installation of Shoppers Calculators in all Wal-Mart Supercenters and Hypermarts. Wal-Mart to validate concept.
10-91	Installations completed in eight Supercenters and Wal-Marts
10-91 to 3-92	ADDvantage Media conducts research involving all store managers and assistant managers.

Results of Manager Interviews:

> Essentially all store managers made same comments:
> "Never have we tried any program that was so popular with our customers — and believe me we've tried many new bells and whistles".
> Not a single negative surfaced in all monthly interviews with store personnel. Only question that surfaced was why does ADDvantage media continue to ask about the program, yet our management has never asked or followed up.

Results of Wal-Mart Customer Interviews:

> - 63% of all Wal-Mart customers use the Shoppers Calculator service.
> - 75% of these customers use the calculators to track their purchases against their available budget dollars. (Note: according to Nielsen data this translates to 47.25% of Wal-Mart customers spend more money in the stores where Shoppers Calculators are installed.)
> - As a meaningful, helpful customer service, Wal-Mart customers rate the presence of the Shoppers Calculators as an 8.6 on a scale of 1 to 10.

4-92	Results of all consumer interviews and management interviews presented to Dave Lienemann and Jim Donald. Numerous follow-up calls made to no avail.
5-92	Survey results presented to Dave Burghart.
6-92	Terms of contract agreed to in meeting with Dave Burghart, Bob McCurry and Barbara Brown, following internal meetings between Dave Burghart and Bill Fields.
7-92	Day before scheduled contract signing Dave Burghart calls to say the deal is off because Paul Higham doesn't want responsibility of selling advertising.

7-92   Meeting with Dave Burghart and Bob McCurry to present potential of Wal-Mart generating $75 to $100 million of new revenue by allowing ADDvantage media to sell the advertising to national advertisers (thereby not interfering with Wal-Mart's existing sources of advertising revenue).

8-92   ADDvantage Media told to install Bentonville Supercenter for a final 90-day test. During this time the program will be visible to Wal-Mart corporate management and Wal-Mart will conduct customer interviews and advertise private label products to determine impact. ADDvantage Media is instructed to make calls on the national advertising budget side of Wal-Mart's vendors — advertising agencies and national ad directors of companies — to determine if the program can be sold without interfering with Wal-Mart's existing sources of vendor funding. Program coordinator is to be Matt Loveless.

9-92   Bentonville Supercenter is installed prior to Labor Day week-end. ADDvantage Media requests and is provided with Wal-Mart store traffic counts and marketing data for use in presentations to national advertisers.

9-92 to 90-day test is conducted in Bentonville store. ADDvantage Media due diligence
11-92   with store managers and customers is all extremely positive. Wal-Mart conducts its own customer research. Results of Wal-Mart interviews are:

- 63% of all Wal-Mart customers use the Shoppers Calculator service.
- 75% of these customers use the calculators to track their purchases against their available budget dollars.
- As a meaningful, helpful customer service, Wal-Mart customers rate the presence of the Shoppers Calculator service as an 8.0 on a scale of 1 to 10. (Note: All Addvantage Media research combined with Wal-Mart research means data based upon over 5,000 total customer interviews. ADDvantage Media data and Wal-Mart research data identical in terms of customer usage and purpose of use. Only variable was that Addvantage Media data reflected a consumer rating of 8.6 and Wal-Mart data reflected a rating of 8.0. By weighting data proportionate to number of interviews conducted, the customer rating becomes over-all 8.48.

ADDvantage Media initiates a concentrated sales calling program on the national advertising budgets of Wal-Mart's vendors. The response by advertisers — to the opportunity to advertise on the Shoppers Calculators in the Wal-Mart stores — is overwhelmingly positive. The program is viewed as a new and very cost-effective advertising medium.

During the 90-day test ADDvantage Media also presents numerous advertising insert approaches to Matt Loveless, hoping to test private label product impact and show methods of using calculators for in-store theming and promotions. All proposals are rejected and inserts are not to be changed, per Matt's instructions. This is contrary to test purpose as outlined originally, but it is assumed that Wal-Mart does not need to verify ADDvantage Media sales data or that of the sales of 75 test products (advertised on calculators) being boosted an average of 13.1%.

12-1-92   90-day test is complete and ADDvantage Media seeks a final meeting with Wal-Mart. Matt Loveless advises us that management is too busy to meet until after the first of the year. However he advises us that the test has been very successful. Wal-Mart has validated our due diligence and everyone is very pleased with the test results. A meeting is set for 2 p.m. on January 5.

1-5-93   Meeting is cancelled in a.m. because only Matt Loveless is available for the scheduled meeting with Wal-Mart management. He again assures us that Wal-Mart is very pleased with the program and that Bill Fields has made decision to initiate program by installing Shoppers Calculators in approximately 500+ stores. He advised us that as a result of that day's internal meetings the only question is whether Wal-Mart or ADDvantage Media will sell the advertising. ADDvantage Media provides documentation of advertiser demand (some seeking as much as 20% of all carts for as much as 90-days at a time). ADDvantage Media further agrees to sell the advertising for a "to-be-agreed upon" sales commission. ADDvantage Media agrees to have contract finalized for meeting now scheduled for 2 p.m. February 4 (after the Wal-Mart management meetings). It is agreed that at the February 4 meeting ADDvantage Media will bring contract containing a "blank" for percent of sales commission to be paid to ADDvantage Media. All other terms will be same as agreed upon in past. It is further agreed that Wal-Mart will supply ADDvantage Media with the following at the February 4 meeting: Store list with manager names and cart counts; number of Sam's Cola calculators to be installed in each store; percent of advertising Wal-Mart wishes to sell and percent of advertising Wal-Mart wants ADDvantage Media to sell — if any.

2-4-93   Only Matt Loveless and Barbara Brown arrive for meeting. They state that all items requested at previous meeting are still being worked on but should be ready to go within two weeks. Contract reviewed and left with Wal-Mart.

2-8-93   Matt Loveless advises ADDvantage Media that internal meeting is to be held on 2-11 and store list, etc. will be given to us after meeting.

2-11-93   Matt Loveless calls to tell us that meeting was held and Paul Higham said, that "he did not want ADDvantage Media involved in any of the Wal-Mart advertising, and therefore does not want to roll-out the Shoppers Calculator service."

2-12-93   C. Hood contacts Paul Higham by letter to apprise him that his most recent decision to cancel the ADDvantage Media program (his 2nd cancellation) is for reasons which are totally contrary to all of the testing and sales direction given us for the past eighteen months. Meeting requested for explanation of change in direction.

2-15-93   Paul Higham contacted by phone and agrees to February 24 meeting with ADDvantage Media. AMG recaps all test data and provides it for Higham via letter.

143

2-24-93	G. Young and C. Hood meet with Paul Higham, B. Brown and M. Loveless at Wal★Mart. Based upon AMG presentation and review of Wal★Mart relationship, Higham expresses interest in continuing program and selling AMG packaged goods calculator concept to vendors. All AMG materials and "can" models left with him for sales presentations. The use of the "credit card calculators" had an especially strong appeal to Higham. Bottom line, per Higham, was that "we can sell any program we want to sell," so we don't need AMG involvement in selling process. "We just need to determine whether or not we want the program." At close of meeting Paul promised to reconsider his decision and "get back with us."
3-8-93	Follow-up call to P. Higham and mailed additional sketches of credit card calculators.
3-31-93	Follow-up letter to P. Higham again reiterating our expense in maintaining the program and requesting a decision.
4-6-93	Higham responds to request for decision by stating in a letter: "I know it must be frustrating waiting, but please be patient".
4-28-93	Higham contacts us by letter advising of his intent to contract with AMG for additional 200 store installations. Wal★Mart is to sell the advertising.
5-5-93	Contract mailed to P. Higham for review and execution.
5-12-93	M. Loveless called C. Hood to advise receipt of contract and to verify that all AMG units could be installed in advance of Sept. 1.
6-8-93	M. Loveless relates to AMG that of all advertisers contacted by buyers to date, only one has declined. B. Brown contacts AMG with contract changes.
6-9-93	Revised contract returned to Wal★Mart for signing. M. Loveless requests that AMG prepare a flyer for use of buyers in selling the program. Sales meeting with AMG to be forthcoming.
6-18-93	Contract signed and returned to AMG.
6-19-93	AMG provides M. Loveless with suggested "letter to advertisers" and his requested ad flyer. Loveless also requests that we forward to him a list of all advertisers (as a result of AMG sales calls on Wal★Mart vendors) who expressed an interest in participating in the program. All materials shipped 6-17-93, including proposed news release.
7-14-93	AMG and Wal★Mart each issue news releases re: new contract

7-29-93	M. Loveless provides us with copies of internal memorandums concerning program. Loveless is contacted to advise him that his memo is in error, stating: "Vendors are to utilize sampling dollars (no national advertising dollars)." It should state (in accordance with all direction given AMG;) "Vendors are to utilize national advertising dollars — but not sampling or promotional dollars which we already access."
8-25-93	After numerous calls to P. Higham as a follow-up to my 7-29 conversation with M. Loveless (since apparent that no corrected memorandum issued) I was finally able to reach him. I advised him that the memo was in error and needed to be corrected. I also advised him that national advertisers continue to call us for program details — and that to my knowledge, two months after contract signing, not one advertiser has been contacted. His response was that Matt was running this program and he didn't have time to supervise him on the program.
9-22-93	Date of last contact with M. Loveless. Repeated attempts to have him return our calls are ignored. His final statement to C. Hood at this time is: "my hands are tied".
9-30-93	AMG contacts David Glass by letter again stating that while we continue to spend monies in Wal★Mart's behalf, Wal★Mart continues to disregard our calls and correspondence.
12-8-93	C. Hood finally reaches M. Loveless (after 20+calls) who advises AMG that P. Higham elected not to go forward with AMG program "months ago". He expressed surprise AMG had not been notified.
12-8-93	C. Hood again contacts D. Glass by letter reminding him of 9-30-93 correspondence.
12-9-93	P. Higham sends letter to C. Hood (in response to 12-8 letter) stating that: "Wal★Mart will proceed no further due to buyers being unwilling to support the program."
12-14-93	C. Hood letter responding to P. Higham letter of 12-9-3 — outlining their "breach of contract" . ✗
1-4-94	AMG receives P. Higham letter which refers to contract clauses — some of which are non-existent.
1,2-94	Gable & Gotwals contacts Wal-Mart in AMG's behalf concerning Wal-Mart's breach of contract. Wal-Mart elects to go forward with a new contract — terms call for AMG to sell the program rather than Wal-Mart.
6-24-94	Revised contract completed and signed. AMG hires sales representatives, prepares literature and initiates selling process.

5

9-15-94   AMG advised by J. Hamilton that P. Higham does not wish to reinstate Supercenter program after two months of correspondence (Note: This is original Wal-Mart contract suspended at time of "60-day Test" in Bentonville store, with intent of reinstating if final test successful.)

9-20-94   Wal-Mart agrees to 6-month contract extension (from 12-month to 18-month time frame). Contract drawn up and signed 9-28-94.

9-26-94   AMG rep advised by Russell Corporation that Wal-Mart buyer told them they would rather Russell participate in other Wal-Mart programs — not the Shoppers Calculator program.

10-4-94   Heinz Promotion Director states lack of interest because Wal-Mart buyers ask them not to participate in "these types of programs."

10-6-94   Procter & Gamble advises AMG that it's in P&G's best interest that AMG no longer be considered a core supplier. AMG has been a core supplier for four years and previously done hundreds of thousands of dollars worth of business with P&G (with excellent product movement results) in grocery industry. Now that AMG has sole on-cart ad program in Wal-Mart, P&G's largest retailer, AMG is denied (canceled) approved supplier status.

10-10-94   AMG responds to P&G questioning reasons for denial of supplier status.

10-17-94   AMG reminds Wal-Mart of failure to provide AMG with internal representative for advertisers to contact (since Maureen Gustafson's departure over two months ago.)

10-17-94   AMG again requests Wal-Mart assistance in advising Wal-Mart buyers of AMG program due to buyer, Brent Hardin, advising Cadbury Beverages that he knew nothing about program.

10-20-94   C. Hood contacts P. Higham asking for assistance in correcting Wal-Mart buyers' negative responses to potential advertisers.

11-1-94   AMG sales rep, Gene Bay, contacts AMG re: concern that Wal-Mart is being negative about program when advertisers — Colgate, Bristol-Meyers, Revlon — contact them with questions and merchandising statements.

11-1-94   Chuck Ginsky, Cadbury Beverages, contacts AMG re: Wal-Mart "Lack of Knowledge" of AMG program. Makes it apparent Wal-Mart never did try to sell the program under terms of last contract (best efforts). And, more important, it's apparent that Wal-Mart is actively poisoning the current AMG program.

11-1-94	Mark Simon, Pepsi, tells AMG that Wal-Mart buyer, Brent Hardin told him: "Wal-Mart previously tried the AMG program, it did not work, and he did not want Pepsi to support the program." Simon further stated that he could not participate in program due to Wal-Mart's directions and attitude toward program. He asked that AMG find out and advise him why Wal-Mart not supporting program.
11-1-94	Bob Vogle, Block Drug, advises AMG that he went to Bentonville to see the Shoppers Calculator program in use. His buyer informed him that Block Drug would be "much better off" running special programs with him (Wal-Mart) to reduce product prices, rather than utilize AMG program.
11-3-94	Gable & Gotwals contacts Wal-Mart in AMG behalf concerning Wal-Mart's effective poisoning and termination of AMG's potential $12 million program.
11-4-94	AMG again requests to have a Wal-Mart representative assigned as liaison for advertisers. It's now been nearly 90 days since Maureen Gustafson's departure and no one is assisting AMG at Wal-Mart.
11-10-94	AMG again contacts P&G asking for response to cancellation of core supplier status.
11-10-94	Gene Bay calls C. Hood to express concern for Wal-Mart's lack of enthusiasm and support for AMG program.
11-14-94	Wal-Mart assigns Russ Robertson to work with AMG on program. Robertson admits he knows nothing about program but intends to "get up to speed." This action is a direct response to threatened legal action.
11-15-94	AMG supplies Wal-Mart with names of six advertisers who have contacted AMG re: Wal-Mart's lack of knowledge and lack of support for the program.
11-18-94	Ms. Anni Gibson contacts AMG to attempt to explain why Procter and Gamble no longer recognizes AMG as a supplier — despite a four-year relationship. As she states, "AMG's presence in Wal-Mart creates certain difficulties for P&G."
12-7-94	Gable & Gotwals requests Wal-Mart assistance with AMG program utilizing letters and phone calls to correct Wal-Mart messages given to potential advertisers.
12-8-94	D. Zeko, AMG sales rep, reports concern that advertising prospects' initial high degree of enthusiasm for AMG program seemingly always decreases dramatically.
12-12-94	Wal-Mart denies "guilt" and declines to assist AMG.
12-13-94	D. Kellner, AMG sales rep, contacts AMG re: his concerns for cancellation of "done deals" with 7-up and Pennzoil.

7

Chapter 19
Wow! What a Deal!

Although I had dreaded telling Sue of the daunting task before her, my most urgent concern was where we were going to get the money to hire Tom. Despite the fact that we, the management of the company, had been working for nothing for several years, the company still had no money. For the previous months we had scraped and borrowed from every conceivable source, and further opportunities appeared to be non-existent.

Tom had outlined his firm's charges in a manner in which we had a choice. Our choices were (1) an up-front fifty-thousand-dollar retainer plus a 25 percent contingency of the lawsuit proceeds; or (2) a twenty-five-thousand-dollar retainer plus 33 percent of the lawsuit proceeds.

Our problem was that we had no money for either, and our immediate thoughts went to how to raise the twenty-five thousand. Then it dawned on me that if we elected to pay the fifty-thousand-dollar retainer, we had eight percentage points (the difference between the 33 and the 25 percents) that we could attempt to sell investors. We immediately assembled an "investment package" which we presented to about ten of our company's original investors. The packaged opportunity was this: for a fifty-thousand-dollar further investment, eight individuals would receive fifty thousand (fifty-cent) warrants plus 1 percent of the lawsuit proceeds. And 1 percent of forty million dollars was potentially a four-hundred-thousand-dollar return. It had a significant appeal and we sold it out almost immediately, raising an additional three hundred and fifty thousand dollars of operating capital, after paying the fifty-thousand-dollar retainer.

Only after the settlement did we hear any complaints about this particular offering. One stockholder asked why he did not have the opportunity to read this special offering document. The answer was quite simple. My response was, "There was nothing to read." This had been an emergency offering and time had not allowed for any documents to be written and printed. This seemed to suffice. But, absolutely none of those who did invest in this emergency offering had any complaints at the conclusion. Not only did they each receive 1 percent of the calculated proceeds, but all were able to net no less than $2.50 on each of their fifty thousand warrants. And, that was the profit if they elected to convert and sell their warrants immediately. If they held on to them, they enjoyed the opportunity of selling them for more than twenty times their cost.

Chapter 20
More Potential Advertisers Speak Out.
JANUARY 4, 1995

The very next day, following our return from "visiting Mars," Dean Zeko faxed us the response he had received from DDB Needham, Frito-Lay's promotion agency. After previously telling Dean that they were very enthusiastic about the merits of the program, (they had scheduled between thirty and forty people to participate in the forthcoming Shopper's Calculator presentation meeting), this message simply stated that "we are not interested in pursuing any promotional opportunities with your company at this time." They had made this decision without the benefit of any knowledge of pricing, cost per thousand or any rate negotiations whatsoever. It was much like the decision made by Procter and Gamble. They, too, simply said, "Please don't call on our people any more." We seemingly had developed a case of the "plague" and it continually worsened whenever we mentioned that we were selling a Shopper's Calculator/Wal-Mart program.

Frito-Lay's decision had also been made despite experiencing very strong sales increases in product movement when using the Shopper's Calculator program in our grocery store network in the past. In fact, Frito's market development manager, Rich Waite, had been so excited about the program that he had written a letter of recommendation praising the significant increases it had given his Frito products. As he stated, "It (the Shopper's Calculator program) definitely contributed to a generous increase in net sales." Despite this, Frito Lay had no intention of having any further discussions on our program.

A callback to Pepsi Cola, to determine if anything had changed regarding their participation, further emphasized Wal-Mart's poisoning of our program. As Mark Simon, of Pepsi Cola stated, "I have talked to my Wal-Mart buyer until I am blue in the face. He sees no value in it. My main concern is to be sure that he is interested in it and that Wal-Mart is behind it. But he is not budging. So, it's a dead issue so far as I am concerned. I've taken it up the flagpole too many times, and always had it 'slammed down' by Wal-Mart."

Another callback to Bob Vogle of the Block Drug Company revealed that his Wal-Mart representative "was not at all enthusiastic about the program." He further related that he had been told to "spend Block's money directly with Wal-Mart on their programs," because "it would do us far more good."

When contacted, Doc Fletcher of Snapple Beverages told us that his Wal-Mart buyer had said that "the program didn't do anything for him." Consequently, he had "made the decision not to participate based on this response."

Chuck Ginski, of Cadbury Beverages told us that he was going to classify Wal-Mart's statements as "a lack of interest." His Wal-Mart buyer, Brent Hardin, had again told him "he did not know about the program,' or he was being coy and doesn't seem to want to be involved in it." As Ginski also told us, "I have the money budgeted, I just need some help to get Brent on line. That is assuming that Wal-Mart is really into it. We think that it is a neat idea and we would like to go ahead and be part of it. But he is just taking this real 'standoffish' approach." Ginski further related, "I can't figure out why. I am just kind of lost." Hardin had also told him "I don't see that this is where you want to spend your money. It is not going to help you sell any more cases one way or the other." Ginski wrapped up the conversation stating: "I'm pretty dead in the water ... but if you can get a level of interest from his side, I mean your people can talk to the VP of marketing over there (at Wal-Mart) and tell them that Cadbury is willing to spend their money on this thing, we just need to get it all pulled together."

Ginski then added, "I am really looking for you to apply some leverage here. I think someone from Wal-Mart's marketing department needs to walk down to his (Hardin's) office and tell him that they have entered into this thing, and if and when someone wants to get involved, he should take a look at it."

During this same month we were copied on a letter from Visa's marketing manager, Sandra R. Perilli, to Wal-Mart's then VP of sales promotion. This letter spelled out Visa's intent to advertise on Wal-Mart's shopping carts during the forthcoming months of February and March. Soon thereafter, this planned Visa ad program was also canceled.

It was this flurry of negative reports from advertisers that prompted us not just to expedite our meetings and communications with Tom Mars — who had since agreed to represent us — but we also purchased telephone-adaptable tape recorders. These recorders were attached to the phones of each of our sales personnel, and they were immediately activated if and when any advertiser called to report a negative response from Wal-Mart, relative to our program.

Not surprisingly, there were many such calls. They occurred on a near-daily basis throughout the months of January and February. In fact, on our very next trip to visit Mars in Fayetteville, we were able to take him nearly three dozen taped conversations — all of which documented Wal-Mart's intent to destroy our program and our company.

The standard line from the Wal-Mart buyers — to their vendors and our potential advertisers — was simple and consistent: "Rather than advertise on those calculators, I want you to give me the money instead. I will use it to lower your prices and it will work much better for you and your products." This was the extent of Wal-Mart's contractually agreed-to 'best efforts' on our behalf. It was as if Wal-Mart had enlisted our services to locate new revenues in their behalf. Once we reported such new opportunities, they were immediately "stolen" from us. And, we were not up against simply one such "gangster." Instead we were fighting their entire "gang."

One of the first tasks Tom Mars assigned us was that we compile an AMG/Wal-Mart Contract and Damages Scenario. This assessment included: (1) the revenues we had lost due to Wal-Mart's negative statements to our advertisers, (2) the far lesser number of stores given to us than required by contract, (3) the three and a half years of testing, (4) the associated overhead expenditures made on Wal-Mart's behalf, and (5) the fact that the timing of their actions had virtually "killed" the chances for success of each of our two AMG public offerings – of three million dollars each. Our list also included our potential loss of both our foreign and domestic patents, due to our lack of sufficient revenues needed to pay the continuing fees and pay outs necessary to maintain them. Furthermore, they had endangered our personal guarantees at the bank, our personal credit, our reputations, and contributed to the past-due payments due our suppliers and our bank — to name only a few.

We, and our program, were sinking fast. We had absorbed far too many shots from the Wal-Mart buyers — via the advertisers who had previously committed to using our program. We now were "near death" and apparently every advertiser or retailer that had ever used or planned to use our program was now aware of our "condition."

NOTE: A copy of our "damages scenario" follows, as well as a list of advertisers that previously used our program in our grocery store network, or planned to do so in the Wal-Mart Supercenters and/or Kmart Super Centers

Chapter 20: More Potential Advertisers Speak Out.

AMG/Wal-Mart Contract and Damages Scenario

1. Contract #1 - All Supercenters - (Signed)
    Value to AMG: $3,250,000 ($800,000 Profit)
    (Per 100 stores per year)
    Currently approximately 100 Supercenters

2. Contract # 2 - All Wal-Mart Stores-(Canceled Day of Signing)
    Value to AMG: $18,000,000 ($6,000,000 Profit)
    (Based upon contractual revenue terms of $18 per calculator per year.)
    Contract was to be initiated, subject to 60-day test which was very
    successful. Contract had been fully approved by Wal-Mart and their
    legal department until intervention by Higham.

    Note: AMG continued to pursue Wal-Mart based upon finalized (one signed,
    one yet-to-be-signed) contracts worth $ 21+ million revenue per year.
    Value would continue to grow as Wal-Mart added new stores.

3. From this point forward — for 3-1/2 years — AMG incurred approximately $10
    million in losses while in pursuit of signed contracts

4. AMG received a 200-store contract even though 500-1,000 stores was the
    fewest number ever discussed. Still, gross revenue potential was $4 to $9
    million. Simultaneously, Wal-Mart canceled contract #1 and proceeded to
    breach this contract.

5. Wal-Mart revised breached contract (existing) and instructed all advertisers
    not to participate. This contract offered opportunity for partial recovery of
    past expenses plus revenue potential of $8-$12 million.

6. Wal-Mart's activities "killed" two public offerings of approximately $3 million
    each. In both cases Wal-Mart was alerted in writing that their actions were
    endangering these offerings.

Walmart's EGONOMICS

1. Stock value altered from $18 million corporation value (at time of initial Wal-Mart test) to $375,000 (at present).

2. Personal guarantees in corporation's behalf based upon Wal-Mart commitments.

3. Wal-Mart's negative comments to advertisers are extremely damaging to future programs ("we don't like it"; "it doesn't work"; "don't use it"). Immense and immeasurable damage to AMG in trying to sell Kmart, Venture, etc. future programs. Advertiser prospects are the same for all programs. Difficult to impossible for advertisers to forget or overlook Wal-Mart's poisoning in the past.

4. Wal-Mart's actions substantially damaged AMG corporate credit and credibility with all suppliers (most important, Texas Instruments and banking relationships). Also damage to personal (Hood and Young) credibility. "We've been banking on Wal-Mart for 3 1/2 years."

5. Our $10 million loss plus the $600,000 worth of salaries and expenses of all contracted representatives who spent time attempting to sell the most recent program.

6. Potential loss of patent due to lack of revenues for pay-out (purchase of all patent rights)

7. As of today AMG would have no ability to perform on any other contract (patent, Texas Instruments, Bank).

8. AMG has also now lost an entire field sales staff and field service force. Any future efforts would require hiring and training all-new personnel.

 **ADDvantage Media Group, Inc.**

Meridian Tower • 5100 E. Skelly Drive, Suite 1080 • Tulsa, Oklahoma 74135
Telephone (918) 665-8414 • FAX: (918) 665-2476

SHOPPERS CALCULATOR SPONSORS

Andrew Jergens Company	Aloe Lotion, Aloe & Lanolin Soap
Campbell Soup Company	V-8, Chunky Soup, Swanson Great Starts
Cantisano Foods, Inc.	Francisco Rinaldi Pasta Sauce
Clorox Company	Hidden Valley Ranch Dressing
Coca-Cola Bottling Co. - New York	Coke Classic, Sprite
Coca-Cola Foods - Cincinnati	Minute Maid Orange Juice
Dial Corporation	Purex Liquid Detergent
Dr. Pepper	Diet Dr. Pepper
Drackett Company	Drano
Frito-Lay, Inc.	Cheetos, Doritos, Munchos, Fritos, Tostitos, Lay's Potato Chips
GTE Corporation	Sylvania Light Bulbs
General Foods	Post Raisin Bran
General Mills, Inc.	Triples, Total Raisin Bran
Georgia-Pacific Corporation	Coronet, Sparkle, Angel Soft, MD Bath Tissue
Golden Grain	Rice-A-Roni
Heinz Pet Foods	Reward Dog Food
Hershey Foods Corporation	Kisses, Reeses Pieces
James River Corporation	Brawny
Kraft General Foods, Inc.	Tang, Seven Seas Dressing, General Foods International Coffee, Grated Parmesan, Velveeta
Lever Erothers Company	ALL
McNeil Consumer Products Company	Tylenol
Nabisco Biscuit Company	Oreo, Ritz
Nabisco Brands, Inc.	Shredded Wheat, A-1, Fleischmann's Margarine
Nutrasweet Company	Equal
Procter & Gamble	Tide, Pringles, Citrus Hill Orange Juice Oxydol, Hawaiian Punch
Pepsi-Cola Company	Pepsi, Diet Pepsi
Quaker Oats Company	Special Cuts, Canine Carry Outs, Pup-Peroni, Gainesburgers, Cap'n Crunch, Instant Oats, Standard Oats, Instant Oatmeal
R.J. Reynolds Tobacco Company	NOW Cigarettes
Ragu Foods, Inc.	Ragu Spaghetti Sauce
Ralston Purina Company	Chuckwagon, Kibbles & Chunks, Grrravy, Bread du Jour, Eveready Batteries
S.C. Johnson and Sons, Inc.	OFF!
Scott Paper Company	Viva, ScotTissue, Sofkins
Sorrento Cheese Company	Sorrento String Cheese
Sunshine Biscuits, Inc.	Super Mario Brothers Cookies, Krispy Saltine Crackers, Cheez-its
Thomas J. Lipton, Inc.	Lipton Tea

Chapter 21

Regretfully, We File Our Complaint.

JANUARY 18, 1995

It was on this date that Tom Mars officially filed ADDvantage Media Group's complaint against Wal-Mart Stores, Inc. He simultaneously sent the complaint to the office of Robert K. Rhoads, Wal-Mart's then general counsel. With this complaint was a cover letter from Mars stating that "my client is still willing to discuss solutions to this problem as an alternative to litigation."

(NOTE: A copy of AMG's complaint is on pages 209-226 of the Appendix.)

Within days of this filing, and the resulting press coverage, we began to receive numerous calls and letters from friends, stockholders and even complete strangers. For the most part, they applauded our courage for going up against "Goliath."

What we did not tell them was that it was not based upon courage; we simply had no choice. But it was readily apparent that should we need any sideline "cheerleaders," we had plenty of willing souls.

Perhaps the strangest message came from a Little Rock, Arkansas, broker, Phillip Cate. Mr. Cate called to tell us that a friend and fellow-broker had informed him that a Wal-Mart executive previously told him "AMG would never

159

be allowed to install its calculators in the Wal-Mart stores because Wal-Mart did not want their customers knowing how much they were spending." This was information given to him nearly eighteen months previously.

Chapter 22
See No! Hear No! Speak No!
FEBRUARY-MARCH

With our complaint filed, our sales people and Tom Mars sought to obtain witnesses on our behalf. Unfortunately, our calls and letters to the many advertisers that had previously planned to advertise on our calculators were fruitless. Despite the fact that we had previously recorded conversations with many of these people — complaining to us about their particular buyer's negative thoughts on the program — all were now predictably "silent" regarding Wal-Mart's oft-stated position on our program.

Nearly all ignored our requests for potential testimony, and in many cases they feigned a lack of knowledge of the program. Even when Mars was able to reach one by phone, that person surprisingly "had no knowledge of the program."

One advertiser, who had previously budgeted two hundred and forty thousand dollars to promote a single product, knew about the program but his company had "never had nor expressed any interest in employing the calculators."

Despite this type of response from our potential advertisers, surprisingly, at least to me, Tom's next action was to send to Jon Comstock — Wal-Mart's chosen, internal, legal-team representative — transcripts of a few of our tape-recorded conversations with advertisers — all of which accurately depicted Wal-Mart's negative attitudes related to our program.

In the meantime, Wal-Mart's responses to the filing of our complaint were quite predictable. Jon Comstock pleaded their innocence.

His response indicated real astonishment among the Wal-Mart personnel involved. In one of his responses by letter, Comstock stated: *"Mr. Higham reportedly was aware of the general issue of hindrance or sabotage, but he was unable to trace it down to any known conduct on the part of any Wal-Mart associate. However he remains committed to working through any contract issues with ADDvantage Media ... and awaits their request to install additional Shoppers Calculators in Regions 2 and 9."*

This quote was perhaps the most incredible, but the additional content of Higham's response provided us with a great deal of entertaining, comical reading.

> **NOTE:** *The following pages are copies of the Comstock response as well as the proposed "cure-all" letter and memo that Higham proposed to send, internally and externally. My personal opinion of this attempt to cure their "destroying our program, and very soon our company," was like saying: "Gosh, we are truly sorry that we poisoned you. Why don't you take two aspirins and get some rest? You will feel much better."*

Walmart's EGONOMICS

WAL★MART

WAL★MART STORES, INC. LEGAL TEAM
702 SW 8TH STREET
BENTONVILLE, AR 72716-8095
PHONE: 501-273-4505
FAX: 501-273-8650

JON B. COMSTOCK
Corporate Litigation Counsel
CHERYL R. EASTRIDGE
Legal Assistant

George J. Bacso, III
Jon B. Comstock
Blake S. Clardy
Allison D. Garrett
Martin G. Gilbert
Glen R. Haas
Charlyn S. Jarrells
Dennis M. Kinney

Robert D. Klock
K. Max Koonce II
J. Scott Melton
Lester C. Nail
Robert K. Rhoads
Deborah J. Smith
Sollie Stroud Varner
Ronald A. Williams

March 14, 1995

Thomas A. Mars, Esq.
Everett, Mars & Stills
P.O. Box 1646
Fayetteville, Arkansas 72702

Re: **ADDvantage Media Group Inc.**

Dear Tom:

First, thank you for your recent courtesy in agreeing to my request to further extend Wal-Mart's answer date an additional 15 days (to March 23), and in providing me transcripts of the four conversations between Cindy Hood and others.

As to the letter you referenced to me earlier regarding a possible sale of the patent rights to the Shoppers Calculator, you have now advised me that you were in error in believing such a letter had been sent to Wal-Mart. Accordingly, I need not address that issue further.

As I previously have told you, Paul Higham in my first meeting with him following the filing of your suit, expressed a complete desire on the part of Wal-Mart to go forward with the business relationship with ADDvantage Media. Though he was aware of the general issue of "hindrance or sabotage" that you raise in the pending lawsuit, he was unable to trace it down to any known conduct on the part of a Wal-Mart associate. He remains committed to working through any contract issue with ADDvantage Media, and awaits their request to install additional units of the Shoppers Calculator in Regions 2 and 9.

I reported to you yesterday my meeting with Bill Fields of the same date. Mr. Fields also expressed complete agreement with Paul Higham's position. He was concerned that while Wal-Mart certainly had not intentionally hindered the contract between the parties, ADDvantage Media had information to at least suggest that the level of internal communication within Wal-Mart could perhaps

163

Chapter 22: See No! Hear No! Speak No!

be improved upon with the intent of fostering the business relationship at issue. With this in mind, I understand that Paul Higham is forwarding to you under separate cover letter (addressed to ADDvantage Media) a draft Memorandum to be issued to all Wal-Mart buyers this Friday, March 17, 1995. If any aspect of the communication is not to your client's liking, please advise by fax by 3:00 p.m., Thursday, March 16, 1995, specifically with the exact wording of any proposed change. Of course I cannot commit to utilizing your proposed language, but am not at all adverse to you submitting your thoughts. As an aside, I am hopeful that you find the draft communication very much to your liking and that of ADDvantage Media.

To further allay any concerns that potential advertisers have been discouraged from participating in the Shoppers Calculator program, I understand that Wal-Mart is agreeable to send a letter to any advertiser identified and requested by ADDvantage Media. We would ask that the request be in writing and directed to the attention of Paul Higham. Mr. Higham is providing you a copy of the proposed letter.

The above actions are being taken for the sole purpose of facilitating the contractual relationship between ADDvantage Media and Wal-Mart. While these actions are not contingent on any action ADDvantage Media may or may not take as to the pending lawsuit, it is hoped that ADDvantage Media will be satisfied as to the good faith of Wal-Mart in this matter and would voluntarily dismiss the litigation. Of course such dismissal could be "without prejudice", thus allowing ADDvantage Media the opportunity to evaluate Wal-Mart's conduct in its proper context.

Finally, to the extent you or ADDvantage Media still desire a face to face conference, both Paul Higham and Bill Fields are very willing to participate at the earliest time mutually convenient for all parties. I have given your office alternative times of this Thursday after 3:30 p.m. or next Wednesday after 10 a.m. I look forward to hearing from you.

Very truly yours,

Jon B. Comstock

JBC:cre

cc: Paul Higham
      Bill Fields

P.S.   I've just learned Paul Higham is out of the office for two weeks starting this Friday, so he is not available next Wednesday. He will be in Monday, March 27th, all day, or March 28th from 8:00 a.m. to 10:00 am. and back on the 3rd of April.

WAL★MART·

Paul V. Bligham   Tuesday, March 14, 1995
Vice President
Marketing

Mr. Charles H. Hood
ADDvantage Media Group, Inc.
Meridian Tower
5100 E. Skelly Drive
Suite 1080
Tulsa, OK 74135

Dear Chuck:

I am writing you for the purpose of clarifying certain issues of concern you have raised with Wal-Mart regarding the Shoppers Calculator program. It is my hope that this letter and the enclosures will satisfy you that Wal-Mart is committed to the business relationship existing with ADDvantage Media and looks forward to the prospects of a beneficial future.

Before the end of last year you had expressed concern to various persons at Wal-Mart that Wal-Mart's buyers were either uninformed about the Shoppers Calculator program or were discouraging advertisers from participating in it. Though you provided me with limited information, I did attempt to investigate your concerns and did not find any evidence substantiating them. Since, the filing of your lawsuit your counsel has provided Wal-Mart's attorney with four (4) transcripts of recorded conversations occurring in early 1995 between Cindy Hood and various Wal-Mart vendor representatives. I have reviewed those transcripts and am satisfied that they do at least indicate that we could do more on our end to communicate with our buyers. With this in mind it is my intention to issue the enclosed Memorandum to our Buyers this Friday, March 17, 1995. In a further effort to assure you of Wal-Mart's good faith in this matter, I am very willing to issue the enclosed "advertiser" letter to any vendor you may desire.

I hope these enclosures satisfy any concerns you may have, and I look forward to going forward in what we all hope is an exciting and beneficial endeavor.

In the future, should any other issues come up that concern you as to Wal-Mart's commitment to the relationship between us, please bring them to my attention. I will make every effort to address them in a timely fashion. My commitment to you is to do likewise in the event any issues come up as to ADDvantage Media's performance.

Sincerely,

WAL-MART LETTERHEAD

DRAFT OF 03/14/95

Dear _____,

ADDvantage Media Group Inc. has advised us that you are presently considering participation in the Shoppers Calculator\Wal-Mart on-cart in-store advertising program. This program is the product of a contract between Wal-Mart and ADDvantage Media Group entered into in May of 1994. As presently defined, the program will be initiated in Wal-Mart's Regions number 2 and 9. Whether the program is expanded to additional regions will depend on Wal-Mart's assessment of the program.

Presently, this program is our sole in-store, on-cart advertising program, and we recommend it to you for your consideration, utilizing your national advertising dollars. As currently developed, the program provides that ADDvantage Media is solely responsible for obtaining the advertising. You should be aware that it is further agreed that the advertising dollars which may be extended by you will come from your national advertising budget, and thus will not effect any reduction of any of the advertising currently available to Wal-Mart.

Based on years of analysis, ADDvantage Media is very confident that their Shoppers Calculator will be good for your business as well as Wal-Mart's. Though the present program was preceded by some testing at Wal-Mart, we are continuing to investigate the potential of this product by the current program. By the current terms, the program will run for at least 18 months AFTER ADDvantage Media is successful in placing sufficient advertising in at least 90% of the stores in Regions 2 and 9. At the end of that period, Wal-mart will evaluate the program for continuance, modification or termination. Obviously, the more participants in the program, the more information we will all have to better evaluate the Shoppers Calculator.

Wal-Mart is hopeful that the Shoppers Calculator program will be mutually beneficial should you elect to participate. If you have any general or specific questions regarding the program, feel free to call the Director of Sales Promotion, who is presently Russ Robertson, ext. 6353, who will be coordinating the program here at Wal-Mart.

Sincerely,

Paul V. Higham

cc: Bill Fields

Walmart's EGONOMICS

WAL-MART STORES, INC.
BENTONVILLE, ARKANSAS

MEMORANDUM

TO: ALL WAL-MART BUYERS

FROM: BILL FIELDS
           PAUL HIGHAM

SUBJECT: ADDVANTAGE MEDIA COMPUTER SHOPPING CART AGREEMENT

DATE: MARCH 17, 1995

This Memorandum is intended to update you on the contract Wal-Mart entered into with Addvantage Media Group Inc. in May, 1994 for a Wal-Mart on-cart, in-store advertising program in Regions 2 and 9. While many of you already are aware of this information, this Memorandum is intended to insure that all buyers are aware of the Shoppers Calculator Program.

While this contract represents continued limited testing of this program, the execution of this contract by Wal-Mart was preceded by testing. The Shoppers Calculators appeared to be appreciated by many customers, and ADDvantage Media believes it has a potential to increase a customer's average transaction and to specifically increase sales of the advertised products. The purpose of the current contract is to allow both Wal-Mart and ADDvantage Media to further explore the potential of this product. At this point, Wal-Mart is committed to exploring what this potential may actually be.

In the past there has been some concern expressed by ADDvantage Media that Wal-Mart Buyers either were uninformed of the Shoppers Calculator program, or were not encouraging Vendors to participate in the program. The purpose of this Memorandum is simply to help eliminate any confusion of your part as to what Wal-Mart's position is as to this program.

Under the contract, it is the sole responsibility of ADDvantage Media to obtain the requisite advertising to be placed on the carts. Wal-Mart in turn agrees to support all such advertising sales efforts by providing to ADDvantage Media or directly to such potential advertisers such information regarding Wal-Mart's locations, marketing efforts, publicly disclosed expansion plans and any other relevant information reasonably requested by ADDvantage Media or any such potential advertiser.

A response that was not predictable was Comstock's attempt to have Tom Mars removed from the case, due to what he defined as being an attorney/client "conflict of interest." This accusation stemmed from Tom's law partner, John Everett, previously representing Robert Rhoads, Wal-Mart's chief legal counsel, in the Rhoads' divorce case. In response to this, John Everett stated that such an accusation truly "boggled his mind" and that he "fully intended to be active in the ADDvantage litigation." This subject was never mentioned again.

At this same time, Tom forwarded to us Wal-Mart's initial set of interrogatories and their first request for production of documents. He further urged us to respond "quickly, accurately and completely to all of their discovery requests."

Doing so was not difficult in view of our having documented and recorded the minutes of each of our meetings — with representatives of Wal-Mart and our potential advertisers. And, in reality, such a step was even unnecessary. This was because copies of all documents had been previously sent to each of Wal-Mart's attending executives at the conclusion of every AMG/Wal-Mart meeting. This had always been done in order to avoid any possible disagreement as to the decisions made in each. Accordingly, we were able to respond almost immediately.

Within a few days, Tom forwarded us Wal-Mart's answer to the allegations of our lawsuit. A cursory review indicated that it was primarily a series of denials and "memory lapses."

NOTE: A copy of Wal-Mart's *response* to the AMG filing is on pages 227-252 of the Appendix.

On April 13, Jon Comstock finally responded to Tom Mars' March 13 request for a meeting between AMG and Wal-Mart's advertising and marketing personnel. He had established a day and time of Friday, April 21 at 4:00 p.m. in the offices of Everett, Mars and Stills.

The following day Michael Warsinske, another one of our sales consultants, notified Visa that they would be unable to conduct their planned advertising program on the carts in Wal-Mart in view of the pending lawsuit. Ironically, this was the sole advertiser that we needed to notify. This was because every other advertiser had canceled due to Wal-Mart's intimidating suggestions that they do so, the majority of which were made by their respective Wal-Mart buyers. In the case of Visa, they were not yet accepted in Wal-Mart, and consequently not considered to be a vendor, despite their hopes of becoming one.

APRIL 21, 1995

Our long-anticipated meeting with Bill Fields and Paul Higham did, in fact, occur as scheduled. It took place in the conference room at Everett, Mars and Stills, and, from the outset, the attending Wal-Mart personnel appeared to have assumed a conciliatory attitude. Though no real admissions were ever made to the charges in our filing, statements were made indicating a "real" understanding of our difficulties and a desire to cooperate with us in the future. Accompanying this new attitude was the request that AMG prepare a revised business/operating plan to include the installation of all current and forthcoming new Supercenters. This time, Wal-Mart was to sell the advertising.

Six days later, on April 27, we delivered the requested operating plan to Mars for his delivery to Fields and Higham. Tom immediately faxed this operating plan to Jon Comstock, and with the cover letter sought a follow-up meeting. This letter follows:

Chapter 22: See No! Hear No! Speak No!

EVERETT, MARS & STILLS

Attorneys at Law

John C. Everett
Thomas A. Mars
David D. Stills

3822 N. Parkview Drive
P.O. Box 1646
Fayetteville, AR 72702-1646

tel. (501)443-0292
fax: (501)443-0564

April 27, 1995

VIA FACSIMILE

Mr. Jon B. Comstock
Wal-Mart Corporate Offices
702 S.W. 8th Street
Bentonville, AR 72716

RE: ADDvantage Media Group, Inc. vs. Wal-Mart Stores, Inc.
       U.S.D.C., Western District, Fayetteville Division, No. 95-5008

Dear Jon:

I understand that you are in Miami today, and I have left a message with Cheryl regarding our availability to have another meeting with Mr. Fields and Mr. Higham. I am writing this letter simply to confirm this message and a couple of other matters.

Chuck Hood and Gary Young came to my office this morning and delivered detailed projections of the revenues to be generated from the Shoppers Calculator program based on the information supplied by Mr. Higham earlier this week. Rather than sending you this information and letting you try to interpret it, I think it would be better to have a face-to-face meeting with Mr. Fields and Mr. Higham so that Gary Young can explain the format he used, his assumptions, and the basis for the revenue projections. I am very encouraged by the information received from Mr. Higham, and our projections, and I am becoming increasingly optimistic that we will be able to arrive at a mutually acceptable and profitable business plan.

Although we appreciate Mr. Fields' offer to come to Tulsa for the next meeting, Chuck Hood and Gary Young are quite willing to come to Bentonville instead. Hopefully, we can have a brief (30 minutes) meeting in Bentonville the first part of the week. At that meeting, I would like to have Gary Young explain to Mr. Fields and Mr. Higham the information that we have put together so that Wal-Mart can evaluate the revenue projections. From that point, I think we can begin serious discussions about putting together an operating plan that is consistent with the projections.

Mr. Jon B. Comstock
April 27, 1995
Page Two

We have assembled our responses to your interrogatories and document requests. The responses are voluminous and have been organized in subfiles in large bankers boxes. I think we have everything that you have requested, and it is available here for your inspection. After you have had a chance to look at our materials, we can discuss making arrangements for having these materials copied. I realize that you may prefer to put this off in light of the pending business discussions. However, you might find it helpful to review at least some of this information either: (a) to evaluate Wal-Mart's exposure, or (b) to identify past problems that should be avoided, if possible, in a future business relationship between our clients.

I want to thank you again for your professional approach in dealing with this very challenging situation.

Sincerely,

Thomas A. Mars

TAM:tcw
cc: Mr. Chuck Hood
       Mr. Gary Young

MAY, JUNE 1995

Nearly immediately thereafter, Comstock notified Mars of the meeting date of May 3, at 3:00 p.m., at which time Jon, Bill Fields and Paul Higham would meet with Mars, Hood, and Young at the Wal-Mart headquarters. I seized this opportunity to explain our proposed plan — in writing — to each of those expected to attend.

This meeting was the first to go beyond continuing debates of who was right and who was wrong. Instead, Fields had very specific requests. He asked that we prepare a new Wal-Mart/AMG operating plan, to include (1) "limiting Wal-Mart's revenue share to 10 percent of the gross advertising revenues," and (2) "develop an advertising pricing structure which would adequately finance AMG through the start-up phase, installation phase and the operations phase of the program from 'now' through December 31, 1997."

On May 11, Gary Young, our CFO, forwarded such a plan, inclusive of fifty-five pages of supportive spread sheets, all of which were in answer to Fields' instructions.

Two weeks later, Comstock acknowledged receipt of their requested plan and, as expected, asked that more time be given to them in order to fully review and better comprehend the contents of Young's submission. Simultaneously he requested that Mars agree to a continuance of the already established trial date — now less than four months away.

Fortunately, Mars held firm, denying a postponement of the trial, stating that a prompt trial was "vital to the company's ability to survive." Furthermore Mars stated that a postponement would not be possible until "we reach a binding agreement of principle on the critical terms of the new contract." He also questioned their latest inclusion, which proposed that AMG secure bridge financing. This was not just a new "wrinkle" in their counter-proposal, but was also an impossibility as it related to AMG's "past due" status — with our bank and other suppliers/creditors.

Wal-Mart's response via Comstock was a request to meet with the officers of F&M Bank. On the surface this appeared to be fine. But in reality, it was just one more delay action, as it had now been two and a half months since our initial meeting, and no real progress had been made. And, today, our financial needs were more pressing than ever.

Surprisingly enough, our bankers were able to stimulate action on Wal-Mart's behalf. It was almost immediately after their meeting with the F&M Bank officers that Jon Comstock communicated the very first willingness for Wal-Mart to work with the bank in solving AMG's financial difficulties. Furthermore, it now appeared that Wal-Mart intended to work with AMG, now and in the future in order to clean up the financial mess their actions and inactions had created over the past four years. But nothing was easy, and new and additional uncertainties began to creep into the settlement dialogue.

On June 15, Tom Mars sent the following letter to Jay Mote, executive vice president of Tulsa's F&M Bank, and the supervisor on F&M's banking relationship with AMG. Tom's letter outlined the terms of what he had heard and believed to be the "agreement in principle" between Wal-Mart Stores, Inc. and ADDvantage Media Group, Inc.

Because F&M Bank's stake in our lawsuit was far greater than any other creditor, it was imperative that the bank agree to and approve all terms of any proposed financial settlement. If they refused to do so, we would have to return to the negotiating table.

Chapter 22: See No! Hear No! Speak No!

EVERETT, MARS & STILLS

Attorneys at Law

John C. Everett
Thomas A. Mars
David D. Stills

3822 N. Parkview Drive
P.O. Box 1646
Fayetteville, AR 72702-1646

tel (501)443-0292
fax (501)443-0564

June 15, 1995

VIA FACSIMILE:

Mr. Jay Mote
Executive Vice President
F&M Bank & Trust Company
P. O. Box 4500
1330 South Harvard
Tulsa, OK 74159-0500

Dear Jay:

The purpose of this letter is to update you on the negotiations regarding the settlement of pending litigation between ADDvantage Media Group, Inc. ("AMG") and Wal-Mart Stores, Inc. ("Wal-Mart"). The parties have reached an agreement in principle, subject to bank approval and a few other conditions, that would allow AMG to repay in full its current and any future indebtedness to F&M Bank, without risk to the bank. As you know from our meeting this morning with the Wal-Mart representatives, Wal-Mart has agreed to enter into a new contract with AMG whereby Wal-Mart will absolutely and unconditionally guarantee the payment of not less than $23 million during the first two years of the contract revenue period cycle, which is projected to begin in the first half of 1996.

The contract will provide for the Shoppers Calculators to be placed in all of Wal-Mart's Supercenters during the contract term. This would include 233 stores by the end of this year, with a minimum of an additional 100 stores each year thereafter. Wal-Mart will be responsible for generating the advertising revenues for the program and will guarantee the revenues based on Wal-Mart's projections of the number of stores to be opened during the term of the contract revenue period. Current projections call for Wal-Mart to guarantee a minimum of $10,022,400 during the first 12-month revenue cycle and $13,532,400 during the second 12-month revenue cycle. These numbers are based upon the minimum number of future store openings and would increase at a rate of $35,100 per store, per year ($300/cycle x 10 advertisers x 13 cycles, less Wal-Mart's 10%) as Wal-Mart adds additional stores.

Walmart's EGONOMICS

We have prepared a comprehensive operating plan, a copy of which has been provided to you. Under the assumptions used in this plan, there will be sufficient funds available to operate the company and retire all bank debt within the initial two year revenue period. The guaranteed revenues would be paid by Wal-Mart directly to the bank, and monies would be withdrawn as needed, with the bank's approval, to operate the company pursuant to the plan. Wal-Mart will agree to contract language that will resemble a guaranty of AMG's bank loan. However, Wal-Mart has made clear that, as a matter of corporate policy, they will not provide a guaranty or letter of credit. Although we have yet to agree upon any specific language, it appears that Wal-Mart would agree to put language in the contract that would acknowledge the bank's reliance on Wal-Mart's obligations to pay the minimum contract revenues (as projected in the operating plan). Wal-Mart would further agree to any other contract language deemed necessary to place the bank in the same position that it would be in if Wal-Mart were to execute a standard corporate guaranty. In my opinion, this type of contractual language would be just as enforceable as a corporate guaranty in the Arkansas courts.

We understand that the bank cannot loan any additional funds to AMG until the company pays all back interest and makes a 10% reduction of all current outstanding indebtedness. We are hoping to structure the new contract with Wal-Mart so that Wal-Mart will make a one-time advance payment of advertising revenue in an amount sufficient to pay the interest and 10% of the principal on our past due loan (approximately $800,000). The remaining indebtedness, and the new indebtedness, would be paid off monthly during the 24-month contract revenue period.

I assume that you will have your own attorneys review the proposed contract language before making any decisions about future loans to AMG. In fact, it would be helpful if we could get some input from your counsel before we begin drafting the new contract.

Sincerely,

Thomas A. Mars

TAM:tcw
cc: Mr. Chuck Hood
    Mr. Jon Comstock

Chapter 23

We Are Being Forced to Pay a Toll to Cross a "Bridge" to Nowhere.

Unfortunately, Tom's understanding — and ours — differed considerably from the understandings of Jon Comstock and Wal-Mart. As a result, Jon felt compelled to send a rather lengthy epistle pointing out their differences of opinion

(See Comstock's letter of response on pages 179-181)

JULY 1995

The established trial date of September 11 was now just two months away. Consequently, for the following two weeks, Mars and Comstock traded a flurry of phone calls and facsimile transmissions, all of which were focused on the drafting of a settlement agreement that would be agreeable to both sides. As a result, on July 5, 1995, the first draft of such a proposed settlement was sent from Comstock to Mars. It totaled nineteen pages in all, three of which concerned the order for dismissal of the forthcoming trial.

Less than one week later, Mars responded to Comstock with his edited version of the Wal-Mart settlement proposal. Shortly thereafter, Comstock met with Higham and Fields in order to thoroughly review Mars' re-drafted proposal.

Their main concern was to make certain that the contract was drafted so Wal-Mart could not be sued again should any of their buyers yet again make negative comments about the program. Mars' opinion of this concern led him to tell us: "I think their position is based on a good-faith concern. **It is hard for me to believe that they would implement the program on such a large scale for two years, have the program working well, and then shut it down in retaliation for what has happened this past year.**"

Despite the appearance of there being a soon-to-be-reached contractual agreement, this attempt was never signed because the contract was conditional upon AMG obtaining the bridge financing necessary for the up-front expense of manufacturing and installing the required number of calculators. As expected, without a guarantee from Wal-Mart, not one of the banks that we approached would even consider giving us any type of loan commitment. F&M Bank, in particular, was far too familiar with the lack of intent and/or follow-through relative to Wal-Mart's previous contracts with our company.

WAL★MART

WAL★MART STORES, INC. LEGAL TEAM
702 S.W. 8TH STREET
BENTONVILLE, AR 72716-8095
PHONE: 501-273-4505
FAX: 501-273-8650

JON B. COMSTOCK
Corporate Counsel
CHERYL R. EASTRIDGE
Legal Assistant

George J. Bacvo, III
Rebecca L. Burkes
Ann Curry Caso
Jon B. Comstock
Blake S. Clardy
Alison D. Garren
Martin G. Gilbert
Glen R. Hines
Ronald A. Williams

Charlyn S. Jarrells
Dennis M. Kinney
Robert D. Klock
Matt Koonce II
Lester C. Nail
Robert K. Rhoads
Deborah J. Smith
Sallie Stroud Varner

June 15, 1995

FACSIMILE TRANSMITTAL ONLY

Thomas A. Mars, Esquire
EVERETT, MARS & STILLS
P. O. Box 1646
Fayetteville, Arkansas 72702-1646

  Re: *Addvantage Media Group, Inc. vs. Wal-Mart Stores, Inc.*;
     United States District Court, Fayetteville Division:
     Case No. 95-5008

Dear Tom:

  The purpose of this letter is to respond to your letter of June 15, 1995, to Jay Mote of F&M Bank & Trust Company. I had called your office earlier, and regret that we were not able to talk before you sent this letter. I will address your letter one paragraph at a time, keeping in mind that we are still in the discussion and negotiating stage. The only contractual obligations which are intended to be assumed by Wal-Mart will be those set forth in a written contract executed by an authorized officer of the corporation. I realize you understand this, but feel it appropriate to insure that my communications with you not be construed as anything other than negotiations. In this regard, I understand from your comment yesterday that you will take on the task of making an initial draft of the proposed contract language. I will commit to review it immediately upon receipt.

  With respect to your first paragraph, generally, in spirit, I agree. I haven't looked at the dollars close enough yet to know the accuracy of your statement, but believe it to be fairly close. I would suggest that the only proviso that comes to my mind is that Wal-Mart's obligation to guarantee any funds would of course be contingent on AMG's compliance with the contract. I trust that this is

Thomas A. Mars, Esq.
June 15, 1995
Page Two

implicit to you and your client. For instance, if Wal-Mart generated advertising revenues, but AMG did not install and maintain the computers and advertising, then that would certainly affect the obligation. While this can all be clarified by the contract language ultimately agreed to by our respective clients, I want to be sure to preserve the concept that the "absolute and unconditional guarantee" is dependent on performance by AMG. Upon reflection, I considered what the obligations of Wal-Mart would be if AMG (which is certainly not implied but a contingency that should be dealt with) were to not even obtain and install a single calculator or advertising medium. I trust you concur that Wal-Mart would have no continuing obligation. Another example of defalcation which would affect Wal-Mart's obligations would be misdirection of the funds to other than compliance with the "business plan" submitted by Gary Young. Of course, this should all be able to be addressed with contract language that clearly states AMG's obligations. The intent of the guarantee is to absolutely assure AMG (and its bank) that as long as AMG fulfills its obligations, then there is no risk that the money stream would be present.

As to your second paragraph, I generally have no disagreement other than to make the point that the guarantee of revenue will be based on actual stores opened during the term of the agreement; irrespective of what projections may or may not have been made. As we discussed, Wal-Mart's current projections may be conservative, but unforeseen events could prove otherwise. I think it prudent that the cash flow be tied to actual opened stores. We can talk about what might be an appropriate time frame for them to be opened to be included; probably at least long enough for one complete cycle of advertising to take place.

As to your third paragraph, I generally concur in your comments. While I don't recall any discussion of a "standard corporate guaranty", I would simply state that the objective seems to be the same, and I would defer final comment until I see your proposed contract language.

As to your fourth paragraph, I think it important to go on the record and state that I believe a clear understanding had been reached at the meeting that Wal-Mart would not agree to cosign or advance funds, and then as the meeting was breaking up Mr. Mote did a complete reversal and interjected an issue that had frankly been put on the table and rejected. Nevertheless, rather than terminate the meeting, we did stay to discuss alternatives to the issue of "bridge financing", one of which was a proposal by the Bank that Wal-Mart make an advance payment as it pertains to past interest and a portion of principal. As mentioned, Mr. Bill Fields is unavailable until June 26, 1995. Nevertheless, based on my communications with others at Wal-Mart, you should advise your client and the Bank that such an alternative is most unlikely.

180

Walmart's EGONOMICS

Thomas A. Mars, Esq.
June 15, 1995
Page Three

In a side conference with me, you mentioned the possibility of ADDvantage seeking the equivalent of these funds in a loan from Arvest Bank. I advised that such an inquiry was outside the realm of my knowledge, but I did not know why ADDvantage couldn't do that. You observed that there was nothing that said F&M was the only source of funds. Currently, I am advised and wish to make abundantly clear to you that Arvest Bank is not an entity controlled by Wal-Mart. ADDvantage should feel as free, however, to approach Arvest or any other lending source, but it would be inappropriate for me to refer you in that regard.

My personal assessment is that F&M Bank could handle this transaction if they elected to, and we structured it appropriately. Their comments about "regulators" has to be discounted somewhat; though I certainly don't pretend to be an expert in banking regulations. In any event, I think it appropriate for ADDvantage to either pursue the funds from F&M or to begin seeking those funds elsewhere. If you want this matter to be able to be wrapped up quickly, don't hold out and delay your efforts in this regard hoping that Wal-Mart will reverse its position and advance funds. Again, I think the length to which Wal-Mart has indicated its willingness to go should be more than sufficient to satisfy F&M, who has an incredible amount to gain and lose by this transaction.

As I do not recall it being clarified that I should send my letter directly to F&M or you, I have elected to send it only to you with the understanding that you will forward a copy to the Bank unless you advise me otherwise.

Sorry you have missed me twice by phone today; look forward to discussing this with you.

Very truly yours,

Jon B. Comstock

JBC/cre

Chapter 24

Wal-Mart's Depositions Are Due!

We were now less than forty-five days from the established trial date of September 11. Accordingly, because depositions were required to be completed at least thirty days before the trial date, Tom notified Comstock of his intent to proceed with conducting depositions within the required time frame.

It was in this specific notification that Tom pointed out "the bridge financing issue is within Wal-Mart's control to resolve, and there is nothing further that AMG can do on that issue."

AUGUST 1995

On August 1, 1995, Mars followed through with his previously stated intent by filing our "motion to compel discovery" with the U.S. District Court in the Western District of Arkansas. On this same date, this fifteen-page document was also delivered to Comstock and Wal-Mart. As a follow-up, the very next day, Wal-Mart received a court order to respond to the requests of our filing within the coming eleven days.

Apparently this communiqué truly hit home, for it was only a very few days until Comstock contacted Mars with the further request that he be given an outline of all up-front costs necessary for a bridge loan.

Our CFO, Gary Young supplied a very detailed and comprehensive list of our immediate needs. They totaled

$1,353,000, inclusive of the past due payables necessary to regain the confidence and support of our critically necessary suppliers.

Despite the on-going dialogue relating to the necessary bridge financing, it was just three days later, on August 4, that Wal-Mart filed for a continuance of our September 11 trial date, requesting a postponement of four months, into January of 1996. It appeared to be "hurry up and wait" all over again.

But, finally on August 15, a glimmer of hope reappeared. Comstock contacted Mars and Young telling them that following his evening meeting with Fields and Higham, **"Wal-Mart is not prepared to grant a bank an unconditional guarantee for the amount previously stated, but is willing to do so for a lesser amount."**

He further stated: **"this would necessitate protecting Wal-Mart with as much collateral as is available ... inclusive of such things as a first priority security interest in the calculators and other physical assets available, contingent assignment of the patents, personal assignments from Hood and Young, and providing disclosure of as much information about the operation as Wal-Mart deemed desirable."**

This facsimile was followed by yet another to Gary Young on the same day. Comstock requested that AMG identify and quantify each element of its overhead. But Comstock further stated that "up to this date I have been unequivocal in my statements to you that Wal-Mart would not be willing to provide an unconditional guarantee for any dollar amount. Never-the-less, given our discussion yesterday, I am willing to explore some limited guarantee that addresses some, if not all, of the factors discussed."

The following day, Young responded to Comstock's request for a detailed "use of proceeds" for a seven-hundred-thousand dollar credit line. In doing so, Young stated that this amount would provide no working capital, but if Wal-Mart's revenues to us were to start after ten stores had been installed, as opposed to the previously specified fifty stores, this change would offset a portion of the financing deficiency. Young further requested that the "start-up phase" be extended and that the "operational phase" commence on January 1, 1997, and end December 31, 1998.

For the next ten days Comstock and Mars exchanged varying versions of the basic contract. In doing so, each was hopeful that the other party would be amenable to their offered revisions. But, towards the end of this period, Comstock's travels caused him to virtually disappear from the negotiating table, prompting Mars to contact Robert Rhoads, Wal-Mart's then-chief counsel.

Mars reiterated to Rhoads that "time is of the essence," adding, "Although both Jon and I were in hopes of reaching a settlement via the new agreement we had worked out over a period of the past few weeks, Wal-Mart's discovery is due on Friday. And, Jon's commitment to 'put the brakes on' for his other matters, in order to finalize this settlement, just has not happened."

Tom further stated, "I have never been as patient, cooperative, or understanding with opposing counsel as I have with your legal team … however it has become obvious to me that Jon does not have the time, or that the Wal-Mart executives are unavailable to give him whatever authority he needs."

He added, "I can not understand why we have been discussing a settlement for over four months and have not reached a final agreement. I have negotiated and settled much more complicated cases in a matter of hours." He concluded his letter by stating "if there is anything you can do to help effectuate a settlement, I would certainly appreciate it."

Five days later, Comstock was back at the negotiating table. This time he supplied us with a list of changes he would like to have incorporated in the agreement. Immediately, Mars agreed to a further extension of the final deadline for answering AMG's discovery. He also incorporated the Comstock changes in the document and returned it for review by all parties. Two days later, Comstock notified Mars of his intent to return his additional changes by noon, and he hoped that the two of them could discuss them at 1:30 p.m. the same day. According to his commitment, an itemized list of 84 changes was delivered to Mars at 11:40 a.m. on August 30. Surprisingly, Comstock's suggested changes were incorporated and delivered back to him prior to 5:00 p.m. that same day.

At 8:45 a.m., August 31, fax transmissions were sent from Wal-Mart to the offices of Mars and AMG. This communiqué contained seven additional changes from Comstock, but also stated the following: "Assuming this is acceptable, please incorporate these changes and I will now focus exclusively on the form of the Guarantee and other exhibits."

Then at 3:39 p.m. Comstock faxed back his approval of three additional changes from Mars, inclusive of two additional changes from Comstock. A final draft was issued, and we in turn notified Mars and Comstock that "the agreement appeared to be very much in order," and we were "prepared to sign the contract today."

During the course of the following week, the "i's" were dotted, the "t's" crossed, and all other necessary peripheral matters were addressed. Finally, with the necessary loan guaranty in place at F&M Bank, the contract was signed by both AMG and Wal-Mart — the latter being signed by Paul Higham, Wal-Mart's now senior vice president of marketing and consumer communications. It appeared as though our past struggles with him had contributed to a significant increase in his internal stature.

Concurrent with this signing, the following joint news release was given to the press. It appeared to be an extremely simplified and condensed version of our lives and experiences throughout the past four plus years of living with Wal-Mart's new culture and the ever-present EGOnomics that appeared to rule the 'beast in Bentonville.'

L. G. ZANGANI, INC.

Penn Plaza, 62 Pennsylvania Avenue, Suite 5, Flemington, NJ 08822
(908) 788-9660

For Release: IMMEDIATELY

Contact: GARY W. YOUNG   (918) 665-8414
         LEONARDO G. ZANGANI (908) 788-9660

PRESS RELEASE

SHOPPERS CALCULATORS TO BE INSTALLED IN ALL
WAL-MART SUPERCENTERS

TULSA, OKLAHOMA, SEPTEMBER 6, 1995...ADDVANTAGE MEDIA GROUP, INC. (OTC BULLETIN BOARD: ADDM) Wal-Mart Stores, Inc. (NYSE: WMT) and ADDvantage Media Group, Inc. (AMG) jointly announced that they have entered into a new contract whereby AMG will install and maintain their Shoppers Calculators in all of Wal-Mart's Supercenters in the continental United States. The Shoppers Calculator is a product designed and patented by AMG, and attaches to shopping carts in retail stores as a convenience to the retailers' customers. The Shoppers Calculator includes an advertising image area within which advertising messages are positioned. The Shoppers Calculator was designed with the two-fold purpose of assisting shoppers while they are in the store and simultaneously presenting an advertising message to the consumer.

On January 18, 1995, AMG filed suit against Wal-Mart in the United States District Court for the Western District of Arkansas claiming, among other things, that Wal-Mart had breached its then existing contract with AMG to install the Shoppers Calculators in certain Wal-Mart stores on a limited basis. After the filing of the lawsuit, AMG and Wal-Mart met to resolve their differences, and both parties made independent investigations of the allegations made by AMG in the lawsuit against Wal-Mart. Thereafter, AMG and Wal-Mart both determined that the alleged breach of contract by Wal-Mart was the result of miscommunications and not any intentional wrong doing on the part of Wal-Mart.

Upon the execution of the new contract with Wal-Mart, AMG has agreed to dismiss the lawsuit, and the parties have agreed to go forward with a more comprehensive Shoppers Calculator program. Under the terms of the new multiple-year contract, AMG will install the Shoppers Calculators in all of Wal-Mart's Supercenters in the continental United States and Wal-Mart will sell the advertising for the calculators during the initial phase of the contract. During the term of the contract in which Wal-Mart sells the advertising, Wal-Mart has agreed to guarantee advertising revenues to AMG in excess of $20 million. At the conclusion of the Wal-Mart sales phase, AMG will assume the advertising sales responsibilities for the program. The program will then continue on this basis for a fixed period of time, subject to reevaluation of the program by both parties.

Charles H. Hood, President of AMG stated, "We are very pleased to have settled our differences with Wal-Mart. The significant revenue to be generated through our new arrangement will allow us to revitalize our Company. We will be able to return to firm financial ground as well as continue doing business with other retailers throughout the world."

-30-

Chapter 25
Finally, a Settlement Is Reached.

In view of the overwhelming amount of documentation — of phone calls, meetings and memos — Wal-Mart settled this filing, in advance of the scheduled trial date, for the discounted amount of $23.5 million. This was the amount of ADDvantage Media's debt, all of which had been directly acquired and expended in making every attempt to honor the Wal-Mart contract.

It represented the dollars required to restore the company's health. It also included the dollars that would be required to install the entire network of Wal-Mart's Supercenters for their forthcoming in-store advertising program.

What it did not include was the impossible-to-be-seen long-term damage that had been inflicted on the company during the course of our multiple agreements with Wal-Mart. But at this point, there was no way to understand or prove what the company's future would hold at the conclusion of the suit.

The settlement stipulated that the monies be paid to ADDvantage Media in equal monthly installments for the forthcoming two years. This schedule enabled AMG to repay each of its suppliers that had believed in the validity of the contract and supported the company in the manufacturing, installing and servicing of its calculator products.

As a further part of this settlement, the Shopper's Calculators were to be installed on the handles of the shopping carts in each of Wal-Mart's Supercenters, inclusive of those currently in business and each of those to be opened in the future.

Wal-Mart was entitled to promote any of its products on the calculators, whether they were ads for their vendors or ads for their private-label products. ADDvantage Media was responsible for managing the program, printing and changing the advertisements every four weeks, and performing all service requirements (cleaning, checking for and repairing any damage done to the calculators, etc.). Wal-Mart was responsible for billing and collecting from its advertisers.

Chapter 26
The Depositions Are Canceled.

SEPTEMBER 12, 1995

It was on this date, more than four years after our introductory meeting with Glass, that our "Stipulation of Dismissal with Prejudice" was filed with the U.S. District Court in the Western District of Arkansas.

OCTOBER 17, 1995

Our first meeting with our newly named Wal-Mart "committee" took place on this day. Those present included the three primary coordinators, Paul Higham, John Hamilton and Jan Mauldin. The agenda included thirteen different subject matters, all connected with the initiation of Phase I, which was scheduled to begin January 1, 1998, just two and one half months away. The most pleasant surprise was that all of the agenda items were discussed in an open, helpful and friendly manner. There appeared to be no animosity.

Chapter 27

Our Creditors Are Repaid, and Most Hit the Jackpot!

The lawsuit had been settled and Wal-Mart's payments to us had been initiated. Our immediate responsibility was to repay the lengthy list of creditors/suppliers to who we were so heavily indebted.

The largest creditor on our list was Tulsa's F&M Bank, which on the strength of our Wal-Mart contract, and our strong personal relationships, had loaned us the money necessary to manufacture and install our products. They were paid in full throughout the duration of the initial phase of our contract. But the list also included many smaller supplier/creditors that had also waited patiently for payment.

Previously we had offered — and the majority of our smaller suppliers had accepted — AMG stock as repayment of our indebtedness. This offer was made at a time when the stock was being publicly traded at fifty cents, making our offer the equivalent of two shares for each one dollar of indebtedness. This group experienced an exceptional return on their investment, for upon settlement of our lawsuit, our stock value immediately returned to more than three dollars per share and continued upward from there. This meant that their return was no less than six times the original indebtedness.

A few had refused our stock re-payment plan, electing to await the cash. This group was paid the full amount of our indebtedness plus interest. But their return was very minimal in comparison with the suppliers who elected to "bet on us" and accept our fifty-cent company stock as payment for their services.

I continue to be baffled by the very few who made the decision not to accept our stock offer, and instead await the cash. It made no sense. If the company survived the Wal-Mart suit, the stock value would definitely increase. If the company did not survive, there would be no cash and the stock would have no value. Although we tried our best to explain the upside of the stock opportunity, we lost every such argument. These vendors sought only cash and believed it to be the single best way to settle their accounts. .

Part VI — 1996, 1997

Chapter 28

Economics Overrides EGOnomics!

Thereafter, for the next two years, we regularly continued to have very cooperative and productive meetings with Wal-Mart's appointed management team. Throughout this time, Wal-Mart's customers continued to praise the program, and the sales increases for the advertised products ranged to a high of 48 percent. None were reported to be less than 8 percent, and these were products not considered to be "normal" household purchases.

Perhaps of greatest importance, we were never apprised of a single negative being associated with the Shopper's Calculator program. It was continually praised at every level – inclusive of Wal-Mart's management, store managers and in-store personnel, and their all-important customers. At no time, during the course of any of our regular meetings were we advised of any problems with the program. In fact, all reports were "unbelievably positive." The sales of all of the goods advertised on the Shopper's Calculators were increased significantly. And, Wal-Mart's customers continued to give our program "rave reviews." There were no negatives.

But unbeknownst to us, the settlement of our lawsuit was not the end of the story. In fact, had we been smarter and, more importantly, known the vindictive feelings our lawsuit had aroused within the ranks of Wal-Mart's top management, we probably would have maintained the program on a minimal-cost basis. Further, we then should have invested our remaining lawsuit proceeds in Wal-Mart stock.

It was then priced in the low forties per share, in advance of its forthcoming splits and price increases. But, hindsight is a wonderful thing, and we had the benefit of none — not even a hint.

Because we continued to believe that our program was of considerable benefit to Wal-Mart, we made the conscious decision to reinvest our lawsuit proceeds back into the Wal-Mart program. We increased the size of our in-store service staff, increased the number of their weekly store visits, and directed them to do everything in their power to make the program as "clean and appealing" as was humanly possible. It was our hope that by doing so, Wal-Mart's management would be so pleased with the program that we would enjoy a "near-lifetime" relationship with Wal-Mart.

Furthermore because of their attitudes and actions directed towards us, we continued to believe that "all was forgiven" and that Wal-Mart now recognized the real value of the calculator program, and the "errors of their past ways."

Part VII — 1998

Chapter 29

EGOnomics Overrides Economics!

At the completion of the initial two years of our contract, Wal-Mart had no obligation to go forward with the program — should they be dissatisfied in any way. We were very much aware of this, and in addition to our further investment spending, we conducted an enormous amount of verification research leading up to the start of this final two-year period. Simultaneously, we were given every indication that the program had been, and continued to be, an overwhelming success — according to Wal-Mart's management, store managers and employees.

This opinion was further verified by Wal-Mart's customers and the participating advertisers/vendors. Each of the latter had enjoyed significant increases in sales of their advertised products. Knowing all of this, we continued to find new ways to improve our program. We added additional service personnel and replaced even slightly marred products. We wanted the program to be absolutely "shiny".

These things we did without obligation, in order to further prove the merits of our program. Store managers and sales personnel repeatedly told our store service personnel that "the Shopper's Calculator program was the most successful program Wal-Mart had ever enlisted."

Our products and our people were praised at every turn. And, because they were, our greed kicked in and we continued to believe that so long as we effectively

did our job, our Wal-Mart/Shopper's Calculator program would continue forever.

But, this was not to be, and all of our over-the-top efforts proved to be to no avail. The only opinion(s) that mattered were those belonging to Wal-Mart's "cult-ruling" management.

We had been forewarned innumerable times that at some point they would retaliate against us, solely because we had the courage and guts to sue "Goliath." And they did retaliate against us, with total disregard for the past success of the program.

It was done, not in a rage, but in the business context of "if the contract were to continue, Wal-Mart was to receive 80 percent of all revenues associated with the sale of the advertising." This left us with a meager 20 percent — not enough to pay for the manufacture of our products, much less the costs associated with their installation and maintenance, and the over-all management of the program.

We, like so many other companies were now experiencing first-hand the pricing pressures Wal-Mart was known to force upon its vendors — only in a much more different and devious manner. Far too many companies attempted to sell their products at the prices demanded by their Wal-Mart buyers, and generally they were not successful in the long-term. Others acquiesced to the pressures by establishing new manufacturing facilities in foreign countries.

Like us, too many of these companies soon found themselves in the devastating position of being unable to meet the demands forced upon them. Unfortunately, we too gave our all, knowing how valuable our product could be for Wal-Mart — if only we could get them to pay attention to the test results attributable to the presence of our products in their stores.

We knew – and they should have, also — that our product was extremely well-received by their entire customer base. It was their customers who rated the value of the service as ranging between 8.5 and 8.6 (on a scale of one to ten).

We had proven, too, that the customers who employed the calculators to track purchases almost always spent more money on their shopping trips.

Finally, based upon each and every research project, whether it was conducted by Wal-Mart or a nationally-known firm, their average transaction size was increased significantly. But, Wal-Mart chose never to quantify or verify any of these major benefits. They mattered not to the larger egos at the top of the company.

What mattered was that our company had elected to file a lawsuit against Wal-Mart. We were later told by several Wal-Mart executives that this was any vendor's "No. 1" sin, especially as viewed by then-president, David Glass. And, it mattered not how wrong Wal-Mart's actions had been towards the filing companies. Like us, most of them had been backed into such a corner that they had no choice but to take legal action in order to defend themselves.

This eighty/twenty sharing dictate may have been a clever business strategy, but it was clearly in violation of the contract settlement terms. Consequently, we filed a second complaint, which included breach of contracts, promissory estoppel, misrepresentation, intentional interference with business expectancies, deceptive trade practices and injurious falsehood.

In a rather predictable response to this filing, Wal-Mart executives chose to defend themselves via an offense of intimidation. Wal-Mart answered our second filing by filing a counterclaim.

But this response was not filed against ADDvantage Media. It was directed personally against the CEO and CFO of ADDvantage Media, Charles H. Hood and Gary W. Young. Wal-Mart alleged unspecified compensatory and punitive damages for defamation. They promised to drop their charges once we dropped our suit against them, assuming we each paid them one million dollars in "damages."

Obviously, we were not forced to pay the damages they sought. We were simply forced out of business. And Wal-Mart's warm and fuzzy "happy face" was nowhere to be seen, then or ever, throughout our nearly seven-year relationship. It seemed as though we had been at war with Wal-Mart forever. And, in the end, Wal-Mart won out.

In addition to "kicking us out" of their stores, their management and their buyers had told more than enough lies — the program doesn't work, etc. — to our existing and future customers that we were ultimately forced to close our doors and terminate the employment of our more than one hundred employees.

For Wal-Mart it was apparently "doing business as usual." And, we had been forewarned of Wal-Mart's usual actions and what was to come, on too many occasions. But greed had played a major role in our refusals to believe what we had been told. In hanging around for nearly seven years, we had allowed Wal-Mart's greed to influence ours. And, in the end, Wal-Mart had accomplished what apparently had been their goal from the outset – the destruction of another company. But, for us, there was nothing routine about the end result. For us, it was not just the loss of our jobs. We had lost seven years of our lives.

EPILOGUE

"It is hard for me to believe that Wal-Mart would implement the Shopper's Calculator program on such a large scale for two years, have the program working well, and then shut it down in retaliation for what has happened this past year."

Tom Mars
Everett, Mars
and Stills

This prediction, made by Tom Mars in July of 1995, was perhaps the only mistake he made throughout the course of our lawsuit. As it turned out, his prediction could not have been further from the reality/fate that awaited us. Just two years from the outset of our new contract, and within a week of the completion of our contracted Operations Phase, we were presented with a new option, if we wished to continue our program. This new option specified that for the remaining two years (Phase II) of our contract, we would be required to pay 80 percent of our ad revenues to Wal-Mart. **We could keep 20 percent.** The final decision had been made, and it wasn't good. **They had elected not to own us, but instead had decided to destroy us**.

Our contract contained the provision that if Wal-Mart was not fully satisfied with the Shopper's Calculator program, they were under no obligation to continue. Wal-Mart could terminate the program immediately. This was Wal-Mart's decision, and according to our contract, "AMG had 60 days to remove all of its calculators from all stores within the Wal-Mart in-store advertising network." They had exercised this provision, and they had done so after enjoying the benefits of the program for three and a half years. Under the pretense of "testing" our program, they had even accepted and cashed each of our checks throughout the periods of their "non-performance."

ADDvantage had spent in excess of $1.5 million researching and validating the products' capability of increasing product movement. The results were very definitive that the program did work, and worked very well. However, when America's largest retailer spreads the word that "the program does not work; it is not worth the money, etc.," this not only impacts the company's ability to sell advertising for the Wal-Mart program, its impact is far more widespread. It impacts all future efforts to sell the Shopper's Calculator program to both retailers and advertisers. Assuming Wal-Mart's messages have been believed — and further spread by word-of-mouth — it destroys the Shopper's Calculator/ADDvantage Media Group, Inc.'s selling capability and business. It destroys the company.

Furthermore, consider the future position of the advertisers who were honest enough to tell us of Wal-Mart's activities and statements negating the program. Many were scheduled to be deposed for trial purposes. Consequently, just how willing would they be to conduct business with us in the future? They probably would not be inclined to do so.

During our final two years of working with Wal-Mart's personnel — management, store managers, and "serfs" alike — we forged many strong relationships. It was these same people who told us that despite the overwhelming number of positive reports from Wal-Mart's store managers and customers, a program review was never conducted.

Neither the store managers nor their customers were ever queried by anyone to determine the program's success or failure. Yet, now we were being told that we could keep 20 percent of all future revenues — to pay all of the costs associated with the manufacturing and maintenance of our calculators, printing the ads and managing the entire program. This was not a margin under which anyone could survive. Not even Wal-Mart.

Their final action forced us to remove all of the Shopper's Calculators from the Wal-Mart chain. This was damaging enough, but the "knife through our company's heart" was the resulting cancellations of the Super K-mart program, and programs for other retailers that were testing the program at the time our Wal-Mart relationship was terminated. It was apparent to these other retailers that Wal-Mart's decision to end our relationship meant that we had not performed in a satisfactory manner. In other words, we were judged to be guilty of product malfunction and/or misconduct purely on the basis of Wal-Mart's decision to end the program.

It was this abrupt and odious action that severely devalued our patents and caused us to close our doors and dismiss all of our employees — not because of performance, but simply because of the vindictive lies, attitudes and egos of the leaders of America's largest retailer.

Today, our company is out of business and our former attorney, Tom Mars, is no longer in private practice. To my surprise, Tom has since made the move to Wal-Mart, where he is now executive vice president and general counsel, heading their legal department.

One can only assume that Wal-Mart's thought process, in hiring Tom, was the same as electing to acquire a competitive chain of retailers. Quite simply, "if you can't beat them, make them a part of your team." But whatever the reasons behind their hiring of Tom, it appeared to be one of their very best decisions, at least of those we witnessed.

We had found Tom's skills, character and integrity to be exceptional. Further attesting to our views was the letter he sent me on November 14, 1995, stating: *"This will confirm that we have agreed to accept as full payment for our legal services rendered and costs incurred in the matter, the retainer paid to our firm at the beginning of the litigation and the 25,000 shares of ADDvantage Media Group stock to be issued. "We waive the 25% contingency fee of any recovery made on behalf of AMG in the referenced litigation."*

How many attorneys do you know that would do this? And, just how well will he fit into a business environment based upon EGOnomics? Only time will tell.

Our experiences told us that even today's Wal-Mart management believes themselves to be entitled to exercise their mean-spirited and oft-deadly business practices. They are a part of the "entitlements" associated with being America's largest and leading retailer.

We can only hope that in the future, Wal-Mart's competitors will not follow their lead. One bully that's known to practice EGOnomics is one bully too many.

APPENDIX

IN THE UNITED STATES DISTRICT COURT
WESTERN DISTRICT OF ARKANSAS
FAYETTEVILLE DIVISION

ADDVANTAGE MEDIA GROUP, INC.   PLAINTIFF

Case No.

WAL-MART STORES, INC.   DEFENDANT

COMPLAINT

For its complaint, the plaintiff alleges:

PARTIES

1.   Addvantage Media Group, Inc. ("AMG") is an Oklahoma corporation with its principal place of business in Tulsa, Oklahoma.

2.   Wal-Mart Stores, Inc. ("Wal-Mart") is a Delaware corporation with its principal place of business in Bentonville, Arkansas.

JURISDICTION AND VENUE

3.   The amount in controversy, exclusive of interest and costs, exceeds the sum of $50,000.00, and there is complete diversity of citizenship between the plaintiff and the defendant. Accordingly the Court has subject matter jurisdiction pursuant to 28 U.S.C. §1332.

4.   Venue is proper in this judicial district and division.

FACTUAL BACKGROUND

5.   By way of introduction, this dispute involves a contractual relationship between AMG and Wal-Mart that spanned a three-year period beginning in late 1991 and

APPENDIX

continuing until late 1994. As explained in more detail below, AMG and Wal-Mart entered into various contracts during this time period to develop advertising revenues through the use of the "Shoppers Calculator," a product designed and patented by AMG that can be attached to shopping carts in grocery and retail stores as a convenience to customers. Wal-Mart intentionally mislead AMG throughout the parties' contractual relationship regarding Wal-Mart's intention to promote and use the Shoppers Calculator in Wal-Mart stores and Supercenters, Wal-Mart acted in bad faith and in violation of its contractual commitment to use "best efforts" in connection with the development of advertising through the Shoppers Calculator, and Wal-Mart intentionally interfered with AMG's business relationships with vendors to deliberately sabotage the program so that Wal-Mart could control and receive revenues directly from the vendors, to the exclusion of AMG. As a consequence of Wal-Mart's wrongful conduct, as described more specifically below, AMG has suffered millions of dollars in damages, and the continued viability of AMG is in serious question.

6.   AMG was organized under the laws of the State of Oklahoma in September of 1989. AMG is in the business of marketing and selling in-store advertising to national advertisers through the use of the Shoppers Calculator, a registered trademark. The Shoppers Calculator mounts on the handles of retail shopping carts and includes an advertising image area within which advertising messages are positioned. The calculator performs the basic mathematical functions and is powered by a solar cell. The Shoppers Calculator was designed with the two-fold purpose of assisting shoppers while they are in the store and presenting an advertising message aimed at the consumer.

Walmart's EGONOMICS

7.   From AMG's inception, AMG planned to market the Shoppers Calculator program to retail chains, principally grocery and mass merchandisers, and sell the advertising space available on the calculators to national advertisers. AMG planned to generate additional revenues from the sale of the calculators to third parties, including independent retailers and international licensees.

8.   Preliminary marketing efforts by AMG established that budget-minded shoppers would utilize the Shoppers Calculator to monitor the total cost of the items being purchased and to determine which quantities or product sizes provide the best value. Research indicated that the positioning of the advertising message on the Shoppers Calculator had a very significant and high level of impact and consumer retention.

9.   As of June 1991, AMG had contractual arrangements with several grocery chains for the placement of Shoppers Calculators. These grocery chains included Kroger Co., Homeland, ShopRite, Publix, Acme Markets, Inc. and Tom Thumb-Page. At the same time, AMG had existing advertising contracts with various national brand corporations, including Campbell Soup, Inc., Frito Lay, Inc., Nabisco Company, Lipton, Quaker, Scott Paper Co., Ralston Purina, and others.

10.   Charles (Chuck) H. Hood ("Hood") is the president and chief executive officer of AMG. Hood co-founded his own advertising agency in 1970 and served a chairman of the board until selling his interest in 1990.

11.   As of June 20, 1991, AMG had 1,808,620 issued and outstanding shares of common stock and 265,250 issued and outstanding shares of preferred stock. In late June, 1991, AMG made its first public offering of the company's securities. The stock of AMG

211

APPENDIX

is now publicly traded on the _____.

12.   In June 1991, Hood had a meeting with David Glass, the president and chief executive officer of Wal-Mart. The purpose of the meeting was to introduce Wal-Mart to the Shoppers Calculator concept and the various benefits both to Wal-Mart and its customers.

13.   In July 1991, Hood met with Dave Lieneman, the advertising and pricing manager for Hypermart U.S.A., a division or company related to Wal-Mart. The purpose of this meeting was to follow up on the meeting with Glass and to provide more information to Wal-Mart about the Shoppers Calculator. As a result of this meeting, Hood proposed to Lieneman a contractual arrangement between AMG and Wal-Mart whereby the Shoppers Calculator would be placed in Hypermart and Wal-Mart Supercenter outlets.

14.   In September, 1991, AMG and Wal-Mart entered into the first of several related contracts, a copy of which is attached as Exhibit "A". The first contract called for AMG to install Shoppers Calculators in Hypermart and Wal-Mart Supercenters for a period of one year upon completion of a 90 day test program.

15.   From October 1991 through March 1992, AMG conducted research involving the store managers and assistant store managers in the Hypermarts and Supercenters where the Shoppers Calculator had been placed. Virtually all of the store managers and assistant store managers raved about the Shoppers Calculators. Not a single negative comment surfaced in the monthly interviews. During the same time period, Wal-Mart conducted customer interviews to determine the level of customer satisfaction with the Shoppers Calculator. Those interviews established that 63% of all Wal-Mart customers used the

Walmart's EGONOMICS

Shoppers Calculator, that 75% of those customers used the calculator to track their purchases against their available budgets, and the customers rated the presence of the Shoppers Calculators at 8.6 on a scale of one to ten.

16.   In April 1992, AMG presented the results of the management and consumer interviews to Lieneman. The results of these interviews were also submitted to Glass and other Wal-Mart executives, including David Burghart, vice president for store planning. On May 20, 1992, Hood had a meeting with Burghart to discuss the Shoppers Calculator program. In a follow-up letter dated May 21, 1992, Hood reiterated to Burghart that AMG was "confident that such a Shoppers Calculator media vehicle within your stores represents an all new opportunity to tap media funds totally inaccessible to Wal-Mart – or any other retailer -- in the past." More specifically, Hood confirmed that the Shoppers Calculator program could be used by Wal-Mart to secure national advertising media funds. Per his conversation with Burghart on May 20, 1992, Hood sent Burghart a new proposed contract to continue the Shoppers Calculator program.

17.   In June 1992, Hood and representatives of Wal-Mart, including Burghart, verbally agreed to the terms of a new contract. By letter dated June 25, 1992, Hood sent to Burghart "clean" copies of the new contract, plus copies showing the changes that had been suggested by Wal-Mart.

18.   In July 1992, Burghart informed Hood that the Shoppers Calculator program had been suspended at the direction of Paul Higham, the vice president of Wal-Mart Stores. According to Burghart, Higham had suspended the program because he did not want AMG involved in selling in-store advertising for Wal-Mart. Higham was apparently concerned that

213

APPENDIX

the program would interfere with Wal-Mart's existing sources of advertising revenue. Later in the month, Hood wrote a letter to Bill Fields, the executive vice president for merchandise and sales and explained that the Shoppers Calculator program would not interfere with Wal-Mart's existing sources of revenues from national advertisers. Thereafter, Hood met with Burghart to further explain these matters. Near the end of July, 1992, Hood also visited about these matters with Matt Loveless in Wal-Mart's marketing department.

19.   As a consequence of these discussions, Wal-Mart decided to go forward with the Shoppers Calculator program with a change in the advertising sales responsibility. A revised version of the contract was prepared whereby the Shoppers Calculator would be installed in the Bentonville Supercenter for a 90 day test period that would be visible to Wal-Mart's senior management, whose offices are located in Bentonville. During this test period, Wal-Mart was to conduct additional customer interviews and advertise private label products to determine the impact of the Shoppers Calculator program on Wal-Mart and its customers.

20.   On or about August 24, 1992, AMG installed the Shoppers Calculator in the Bentonville Supercenter. At approximately the same time, Wal-Mart provided AMG with store traffic counts and marketing data for use by AMG in making presentations to national advertisers. By this time, Loveless had become the key contact person for AMG.

21.   The Shoppers Calculator was enthusiastically received by the Bentonville Supercenter store manager. In late August and early September 1992, a Wal-Mart store manager from Mississippi contacted AMG to find out how he could get the Shoppers Calculator placed in his store.

214

Walmart's EGONOMICS

JAN 16 '95 10:40AM EVERETT, MARS & STILLS   P.8

ATTORNEY/CLIENT PRIVILEGED

22.   On September 24, 1992, Hood wrote to Loveless requesting answers to questions that had been posed to Loveless in July and August. This information was required in order for AMG to sell the program on the national advertising budgets of Wal-Mart's vendors.

23.   From September through December 1992, AMG conducted a concentrated sales calling program on the national advertising accounts of Wal-Mart's vendors.   The response of the vendors was overwhelmingly positive. During this time period, AMG presented numerous advertising insert approaches to Loveless for use in the test program at the Bentonville Supercenter. Loveless rejected all of the proposals, leading AMG to believe that Wal-Mart did not need to verify AMG's sales data.

24.   The 90 day test period at the Bentonville Supercenter was completed in early December 1992. Immediately thereafter, Hood contacted Loveless to set up a meeting with Wal-Mart to discuss the program. During this conversation, Loveless told Hood that Wal-Mart had validated AMG's sales data and that Wal-Mart's executive management was very pleased with the results of the test program. Loveless further told Hood that Wal-Mart's senior management executives were too busy to meet with AMG until after the holidays. A meeting was scheduled on January 5, 1993. Prior to the meeting, Hood provided Wal-Mart with additional information about the results of the test program.

25.   In the morning of January 5, 1993, Loveless called Hood to cancel the meeting because certain senior management executives were unavailable. During this conversation, Loveless told Hood that Wal-Mart was very pleased with the program and that Fields had made a decision to have the Shoppers Calculator installed in more than 500 stores. Loveless

215

APPENDIX

told Hood that, as a result of internal meetings held earlier in the day, the only question remaining was whether Wal-Mart or AMG would sell the advertising.

26.   On January 8, 1993, Hood wrote a letter to Loveless providing additional information about the program and making suggestions about how to allocate the costs associated with selling advertising. Another meeting was scheduled for February 4, 1993, and Hood emphasized the importance of Wal-Mart providing certain information at that meeting so that the program could move forward.

27.   Only Loveless and Barbara Brown showed up at the meeting on February 4, 1993. (Brown also worked in Wal-Mart's marketing department.) During this meeting, Loveless and Brown told Hood that Wal-Mart was still working on getting the information that had been requested by Hood. They said that Wal-Mart should be ready to move forward within two weeks. Hood discussed with Loveless and Brown the terms of a new contract. Hood confirmed some of these discussions in a letter to Brown dated February 5, 1993.

28.   In a letter to Fields dated February 9, 1993, Hood thanked Fields for Wal-Mart's decision to allow AMG to begin installing the Shoppers Calculator in more Wal-Mart stores. In a letter to Loveless of the same date, Hood thanked Loveless for calling on February 8th and confirmed that Loveless would be calling back later in the week with the needed information that had not yet been provided.

29.   On February 11, 1993, much to Hood's surprise, Loveless telephone Hood to tell him the results of a meeting involving Higham. According to Loveless, Higham said that "he did not want AMG involved in any of the Wal-Mart advertising, and therefore, did

216

Walmart's EGONOMICS

not want to roll out the Shoppers Calculator's service."

30.   On February 12, 1993, Hood wrote a letter to Higham expressing surprise about his decision in light of the test results and the representations that had been made by various representatives of Wal-Mart about Wal-Mart's intention to go forward with the program. Hood requested a meeting with Higham to discuss the status of the program.

31.   On February 15, 1993, Hood contacted Higham by telephone. During this conversation, Higham agreed to meet with Hood on February 24, 1993. On February 16, 1993, Hood wrote a letter to Higham confirming the meeting and providing additional information about the program.   In this letter, Hood confirmed that Higham's position regarding AMG selling advertising was "totally contrary to the testing direction given to us last August."

32.   On September 24, 1993, Hood met with Higham, Loveless, and Brown. Also present at the meeting was Gary Young, one of the executive vice presidents of AMG. During this meeting, Higham expressed an interest in continuing the program and selling AMG's "packaged goods" calculator concept to vendors. The use of "credit card calculators" was especially appealing to Higham. At the close of the meeting, Higham promised to reconsider his decision and "get back with" AMG.

33.   On February 25, 1993, Hood wrote a letter to Higham enclosing a recap of all the research on the use of the Shoppers Calculator in Wal-Mart stores. Hood further said that he would contact Higham on March 3, 1993, for the purpose of continuing their discussions. After several unsuccessful efforts to reach Higham by telephone, and after several telephone calls were not returned, Hood was able to reach Higham by telephone

217

APPENDIX

on March 8, 1993. In this conversation Higham told Hood that Wal-Mart's buyers were "unwilling to mess with the calculators," but that Visa and Discovery cards might be interested in the program. Hood asked Higham whether Wal-Mart had done anything to determine the calculator's impact on Wal-Mart's sales. Higham responded by saying it would be impossible to make such a determination. The same day, Hood wrote another letter to Higham enclosing sketches that might be helpful in soliciting the Visa and Discovery card accounts.

34.   On March 31, 1993, Hood wrote another letter to Higham in which he outlined Wal-Mart's failure to get back in touch with AMG and Wal-Mart's contradictory instructions and statements regarding the program. In this letter, Hood requested an immediate commitment from Wal-Mart about the future of the program. Higham responded to this letter by letter dated April 6, 1993. Higham told Hood that he was "still working with the potential resources." Higham also said "I know it must be frustrating waiting. Please be patient."

35.   On April 28, 1993, Higham wrote to Hood stating Wal-Mart's intention to place the Shoppers Calculator in "an additional 200 stores for continuation of our on-going test." In this letter, Higham said that the "sole factor for final approval will be the judgment of our buyers as to whether or not the cost of advertising on the calculators will have any deleterious effect on our cost of goods." Higham said that Loveless would be the "primary contact" with AMG and that Brown would be the "executive sponsor."

36.   By letter dated May 5, 1993, Hood enclosed an updated version of the contract that was originally agreed upon on in June 1992, with the changes necessary to

Walmart's EGONOMICS

make the contract current.

37.   On May 5, 1993, Loveless called Hood and told him that Wal-Mart had already begun selling advertising for the Shoppers Calculator program and needed the contract with AMG to be signed as soon as possible.

38.   On June 8, 1993, Loveless contacted Hood by telephone and told him that of all the advertisers contacted by Wal-Mart, only one had declined, and the response from the others was quite positive.

39.   After further discussions between Hood and Loveless regarding the status of the contract, the second in the series of contracts between AMG and Wal-Mart was executed on or about June 28, 1993. A copy of this contract is attached Exhibit "B".

40.   On July 29, 1993, Loveless provided AMG with an internal Wal-Mart memo authored by Loveless regarding the Shoppers Calculator program, which memo had been copied to Higham and Brown. Among other things, the memo said "vendors are to utilize sampling dollars (no national advertising dollars)." Hood contacted Loveless the same day to tell him that this statement in the memo was contrary to the statements made by other Wal-Mart representatives, including Higham, in that vendors were to utilize national advertising dollars -- not sampling or promotional dollars to which Wal-Mart already had access.

41.   Thereafter, after several unsuccessful attempts, Hood reached Higham by telephone on August 25, 1993 and advised Higham that the memo was in error. Hood also advised Higham that national advertisers were continuing to call AMG for program details and that, two months after the contract had been signed, it appeared that Wal-Mart had not

APPENDIX

contacted any of the national advertisers. Higham responded by telling Hood that Loveless was running the program and that Higham did not have time to supervise him. Hood wrote a letter to Higham the same day confirming that numerous national advertisers had contacted AMG and had stated their desire to advertise in Wal-Mart stores using the Shoppers Calculator.

42.   On September 10, 1993, Cindy Hood of AMG spoke with Loveless and was informed that Wal-Mart's buyers had asked for additional time to negotiate the Shoppers Calculator advertising contracts. Loveless told Cindy Hood that he was sending a memo to all Wal-Mart buyers extending their deadline to September 22, 1993.   During the next week, Cindy Hood unsuccessfully attempted to reach Loveless by telephone several times to get an update on the status of the Shoppers Calculator program. Cindy Hood eventually reached Loveless on September 21, 1993. Loveless told Cindy Hood that he would check on the status of the program and call her back later in the day. Loveless did not call back. On September 22, 1993, Cindy Hood telephone Loveless again regarding the status of the contact with national advertisers. Loveless said that he would provide this information to AMG in a few days. When Cindy Hood requested the list of 200 additional stores for planning purposes, Loveless told Cindy Hood that "his hands were tied" and that AMG could not get the list until the ads were sold.

43.   On September 30, 1993, Hood wrote another letter to Glass stating that Wal-Mart had not made any efforts to sell the program, much less the "best efforts" that were required by the contract.

220

44.   On December 8, 1993, after more than 20 unsuccessful efforts to reach Loveless by telephone, Cindy Hood made contact with Loveless by phone and asked him about the status of the program. Loveless acted very surprised that AMG had not previously been contacted by Higham. Loveless was under the impression that Higham had contacted AMG several months earlier to inform AMG of Wal-Mart's decision not to go forward with the Shoppers Calculator program. Loveless told Cindy Hood again that "his hands were tied." He said, however, that he would contact Higham and get back in touch with Cindy Hood. Loveless never called back.

45.   On December 8, 1993, Hood wrote to Glass and asked Glass to have someone contact AMG immediately regarding the status of the program. Hood once again told Glass that Wal-Mart had not contacted any advertisers in an effort to sell the program. Hood further explained that AMG was continuing to spend tens of thousands of dollars each month maintaining the program in the original test stores, that AMG had spent hundreds of thousands of dollars on research, installation, and maintenance, and that Wal-Mart's failure to perform its obligations under the contract were causing a delay in a $2 million private placement for capital by AMG.

46.   On December 9, 1993, Higham wrote to Hood and acknowledged that he had met with Glass to discuss Hood's letter of December 8, 1993. Higham said that "we continue to believe that our decision not to participate is in our best interest." Higham said that Loveless would work with AMG in the process of removing the calculators from the Wal-Mart stores.

APPENDIX

47.   On December 14, 1993, Hood wrote a letter to Higham alleging that Wal-Mart had purposely mislead AMG and had breached its contractual obligation to use best efforts to sell the program. Higham responded to Hood in a letter dated December 28, 1993, stating that Wal-Mart had acted in accordance with its contractual obligations and in good faith.

48.   In early January 1994, AMG's counsel, Gable & Gotwals of Tulsa, contacted Wal-Mart and threatened legal action if Wal-Mart was not willing to promptly meet and reconsider its position, as outlined in Higham's letter of December 28, 1993. Thereafter, a meeting was held with members of Wal-Mart's legal department. As a result of these discussions, Wal-Mart reversed its position and stated its intent to proceed with the Shoppers Calculator program. Discussions, negotiations, and correspondence regarding a new contractual arrangement occurred throughout the first half of 1994.

49.   On or about June 24, 1994, AMG and Wal-Mart entered into the third in the series of contracts regarding the Shoppers Calculator program. A copy of this contract is attached as Exhibit "C". Among other things, this contract contained a provision obligating Wal-Mart to support all advertising sales efforts by providing information to AMG and/or potential advertisers. Under the terms of this contract, the Shoppers Calculator was to be installed and maintained in the Bentonville Supercenter and all of Wal-Mart's stores located in Regions 2 and 9 (comprising over 220 stores in Texas, Arkansas, and Oklahoma).

50.   On September 28, 1994, by mutual agreement, AMG and Wal-Mart entered into a first amendment to the third contract that was executed in June, 1994. The purpose of the amendment was to extend the term of the contract from 12 months to 18 months.

222

Walmart's EGONOMICS

51.   Beginning in September 1994, AMG learned from various third parties that Wal-Mart buyers were actively and specifically discouraging vendors from participating in the Shoppers Calculator program. For example, a representative of Russell Corporation stated that a Wal-Mart buyer had said that Wal-Mart preferred that Russell Corporation participate in other Wal-Mart programs, not the Shoppers Calculator program. The director of promotions for Hienz expressed a lack of interest in the Shoppers Calculator program because Wal-Mart buyers had asked Heinz not to participate in "these types of programs." A representative of Proctor & Gamble Co. similarly stated that AMG could not become a core supplier for Proctor & Gamble's in-store advertising program with Wal-Mart. (AMG had previously been on Proctor & Gamble's core supplier list.) AMG sales representative Gene Day contacted Hood on November 1, 1994, and related his feeling that Wal-Mart was deliberately sabotaging the Shoppers Calculator program. The same day, Cadbury beverages contacted AMG and related that a Wal-Mart buyer had specifically told Cadbury not to participate in the program. The buyer refused to give Cadbury a specific reason why Wal-Mart did not want Cadbury to participate. A representative of Pepsi Cola was told by a Wal-Mart buyer that the Shoppers Calculator program did not work and that Wal-Mart did not want Pepsi Cola to participate in the program. A representative of Block Drug Company was told by a Wal-Mart buyer that Block Drug Company would be much better off running special programs with Wal-Mart instead of participating in the Shoppers Calculator program.

52.   After hearing and documenting such conversations, AMG contacted Wal-Mart and expressed concern with the information that was being provided to vendors by Wal-Mart buyers. AMG requested assistance from Wal-Mart to clarify to potential advertisers

APPENDIX

Wal-Mart's position regarding the Shoppers Calculator program.   Wal-Mart refused to provide any such information to potential advertisers. Wal-Mart's actions in late 1994 have destroyed the Shoppers Calculator program through Wal-Mart and have seriously jeopardized AMG's ability to market the product through other retail chains.

CLAIMS FOR RELIEF

Count I: Misrepresentation

53.   Wal-Mart made false representations of material fact to AMG.

54.   Wal-Mart knew or believed that such representations were false or did not have a sufficient basis of information to make such representations.

55.   Wal-Mart made such false representations for the purpose of inducing AMG to forego legal action, to continue to spend and raise substantial sums of money on the Shoppers Calculator program, and to induce AMG to enter into another written contract, all to the benefit of Wal-Mart and the detriment of AMG.

56.   AMG justifiably relied upon the representations of Wal-Mart in deciding to forego legal action, in deciding to spend and raise substantial sums of money on the Shoppers Calculator program, and in deciding to enter into written contracts with Wal-Mart. As a consequence, AMG suffered damages in an amount to be determined at trial.

Count II: Breach of Contract

57.   AMG and Wal-Mart had a contractual relationship, as evidenced by the series of related contracts between the parties, all of which should be considered as a matter of law to be a single, integrated contract.

224

JAN 16 '95 10:45AM EVERETT, MARS & STILLS   P.18

58.   Wal-Mart breached its obligations under the contracts by violating both the written terms of the contracts and the implied obligation to deal with AMG in good faith.

59.   At the time of contracting with AMG, Wal-Mart knew that a breach of the contractual agreement by Wal-Mart would result in substantial consequential damages to AMG and its shareholders. Wal-Mart tacitly agreed to be responsible for such damages in the event of a breach of the agreement by Wal-Mart.

60.   Wal-Mart's breach of its contractual agreement with AMG resulted in damages to AMG in an amount to be determined at trial.

Count III: Intentional/Negligent Interference

61.   AMG had valid contractual relationships and/or business expectancies with third-party vendors, the identity of which was known to Wal-Mart.

62.   Wal-Mart had knowledge of such contractual relationships and/or business expectancies.

63.   By intentional and/or negligent interference with such contractual relationships and business expectancies, Wal-Mart caused a disruption and, in some cases, a termination of the contractual relationships and business expectancies of AMG.

64.   The intentional/negligent disruption of such contractual relationships and business expectancies of AMG was a proximate cause of damages that have been suffered by AMG, in an amount to be determined at trial.

WHEREFORE, AMG requests a trial by jury and requests judgment on its complaint as follows:

1.   An award of compensatory damages in excess of $_____.

225

APPENDIX

2.   An award of punitive damages in excess of $_____.

3.   An award of AMG's attorney's fees pursuant to Ark. Code Ann. §16-22-308.

4.   An award of costs.

5.   All other relief to which AMG may be entitled.

Respectfully submitted,

EVERETT, MARS & STILLS
Attorneys at Law
P. O. Box 1646
Fayetteville, AR 72702-1646
(501) 443-0292

BY: _____

     Thomas A. Mars
     Bar No. 86115

MAR 27 '95 01:42PM EVERETT, MARS & STILLS

P.4

IN THE UNITED STATES DISTRICT COURT
WESTERN DISTRICT OF ARKANSAS
FAYETTEVILLE DIVISION

ADDVANTAGE MEDIA GROUP, INC.	)	
	)	
Plaintiff,	)	Case No. 95-5008
	)	
vs.	)	
	)	
WAL-MART STORES, INC.,	)	
	)	
Defendant.	)	

ANSWER OF DEFENDANT, WAL-MART STORES, INC.

The Defendant, Wal-Mart Stores, Inc., (hereinafter "Wal-Mart"), for its Answer to the Complaint of the Plaintiff (referred to hereinafter as "AMG"), states as follows:

AMG'S ALLEGATIONS OF PARAGRAPH 1

ADDvantage Media Group, Inc. ("AMG") is an Oklahoma corporation with its principal place of business in Tulsa, Oklahoma.

WAL-MART'S ANSWER TO PARAGRAPH 1

As to paragraph 1 of the Complaint, Wal-Mart admits the allegations therein.

AMG'S ALLEGATIONS OF PARAGRAPH 2

Wal-Mart Stores, Inc. ("Wal-Mart") is a Delaware corporation with its principal place of business in Bentonville, Arkansas.

WAL-MART'S ANSWER TO PARAGRAPH 2

As to paragraph 2 of the Complaint, Wal-Mart admits the allegations therein.

AMG'S ALLEGATIONS OF PARAGRAPH 3

227

APPENDIX

The amount in controversy, exclusive of interest and costs, exceeds the sum of $50,000.00, and there is complete diversity of citizenship between the Plaintiff and the Defendant. Accordingly, the Court has subject matter jurisdiction pursuant to 28 U.S.C. §1332.

WAL-MART'S ANSWER TO PARAGRAPH 3

As to paragraph 3 of the Complaint, Wal-Mart admits the allegations therein.

AMG'S ALLEGATIONS OF PARAGRAPH 4

Venue is proper in this judicial district and division.

WAL-MART'S ANSWER TO PARAGRAPH 4

As to paragraph 2 of the Complaint, Wal-Mart admits the allegations therein.

AMG'S ALLEGATIONS OF PARAGRAPH 5

By way of introduction, this dispute involves a contractual relationship between AMG and Wal-Mart that spanned a three-year period beginning in late 1991 and continuing through the present. As explained in more detail below, AMG and Wal-Mart entered into various contracts during this time period to develop advertising revenues through the use of the "Shoppers Calculator," a product designed and patented by AMG that can be attached to shopping carts in retail stores as a convenience to customers. Wal-Mart intentionally mislead AMG throughout the parties' contractual relationship regarding Wal-Mart's intention to promote and use the Shoppers Calculator in Wal-Mart stores and Supercenters, Wal-Mart acted in bad faith and in violation of its contractual commitment to use "best efforts" in connection with the development of advertising through the Shoppers Calculator, and Wal-Mart intentionally interfered with AMG's business relationships with vendors to deliberately sabotage the program so that Wal-Mart could control and receive revenues directly from the vendors, to the exclusion of AMG. As a consequence of Wal-Mart's wrongful conduct, as described more specifically below, AMG has suffered millions of dollars in damages, and the continued viability of AMG is in serious question.

WAL-MART'S ANSWER TO PARAGRAPH 5

228

Wal-Mart agrees that a certain contractual relationship has existed between AMG and Wal-Mart for a period of time relating to a program referred to as the "Shopper's Calculator". Wal-Mart denies all other allegations of this paragraph.

AMG'S ALLEGATIONS OF PARAGRAPH 6

AMG was organized under the laws of the State of Oklahoma in September of 1989. AMG is in the business of marketing and selling in-store advertising to national advertisers through the use of the Shoppers Calculator, a registered trademark. The Shoppers Calculator mounts on the handles of retail shopping carts and includes an advertising image area within which advertising messages are positioned. The calculator performs the basic mathematical functions and is powered by a solar cell. The Shoppers Calculator was designed with the three-fold purpose of assisting shoppers while they are in the store, presenting an advertising message aimed at the consumer, and contributing to an increase in the retailer's total sales.

WAL-MART'S ANSWER TO PARAGRAPH 6

Wal-Mart agrees that the Statement of Facts contained in paragraph 6 are representations made by AMG to it, and not being aware of any information to the contrary, Wal-Mart admits the allegation. However, Wal-Mart reserves the right to amend it's answer, if during discovery, information is learned which would make this admission inappropriate.

AMG'S ALLEGATIONS OF PARAGRAPH 7

From AMG's inception, AMG planned to market the Shoppers Calculator program to retail chains, principally grocery and mass merchandisers, and sell the advertising space available on the calculators to national advertisers. AMG planned to generate additional revenues from the sale of the calculators to third parties, including independent retailers and international licensees.

WAL-MART'S ANSWER TO PARAGRAPH 7

Wal-Mart admits that it understood AMG planned to market the Shoppers' calculator to retail chains and to sell advertising space to national advertisers. There are many portions of the paragraph which are denied in that Wal-Mart does not have first hand knowledge as to the internal plans of AMG.

229

APPENDIX

AMG'S ALLEGATIONS OF PARAGRAPH 8

Preliminary marketing efforts by AMG established that budget-minded shoppers would utilize the Shoppers Calculator to monitor the total cost of the items being purchased and to determine which quantities or product sizes provide the best value. Research indicated that the positioning of the advertising message on the Shoppers Calculator had a very significant and high level of impact and consumer retention.

WAL-MART'S ANSWER TO PARAGRAPH 8

Wal-Mart admits that the allegations of paragraph 8 represent contentions made by AMG , but Wal-Mart is without independent knowledge to either admit or deny the allegations and strict proof would be required thereof. Accordingly, the allegations are deemed denied. Wal-Mart does acknowledge that it was aware that many consumers indicated in surveys that they enjoyed the convenience of the calculator.

AMG'S ALLEGATIONS OF PARAGRAPH 9

As of June, 1991, AMG had contractual arrangements with several grocery chains for the placement of Shoppers Calculators. These grocery chains, among others, included Kroger Co., Homeland, Publix, Acme Markets, Inc. and Tom Thumb-Page. At the same time, AMG had existing advertising contracts with various national brand corporations, including Campbell Soup, Inc., Frito Lay, Inc., Nabisco Company, Lipton, Quaker, Scott Paper Co., Ralston Purina, and others.

WAL-MART'S ANSWER TO PARAGRAPH 9

Wal-Mart is without any knowledge of the allegations found in paragraph 9, and therefore, they are deemed denied.

AMG'S ALLEGATIONS OF PARAGRAPH 10

Charles (Chuck) H. Hood ("Hood") is the president and chief executive officer of AMG. Hood co-founded his own advertising agency in 1970 and served a (sic) chairman of the board until selling his interest in 1990.

WAL-MART'S ANSWER TO PARAGRAPH 10

Wal-Mart admits that the allegations of paragraph 10 were representations made to it by the plaintiff. Not being aware of any fact to the contrary, Wal-Mart admits the allegations thereof with the proviso that should discovery indicate any aspect of the paragraph be denied, Wal-Mart reserves the right to amend this portion of its answer.

AMG'S ALLEGATIONS OF PARAGRAPH 11

As of June 20, 1991, AMG had 1,808,620 issued and outstanding shares of common stock and 265,250 issued and outstanding shares of preferred stock. In late June, 1991, AMG made its first public offering of the company's securities. The stock of AMG is now publicly traded on the OTC Bulletin Board.

WAL-MART'S ANSWER TO PARAGRAPH 11

Without conducting independent research, Wal-Mart is without information or knowledge to allow us to admit or deny the allegations of paragraph 11, and they are therefore, deemed denied.

AMG'S ALLEGATIONS OF PARAGRAPH 12

In June, 1991, Hood had a meeting with David Glass, the president and chief executive officer of Wal-Mart. The purpose of the meeting was to introduce Wal-Mart to the Shoppers Calculator concept and the various benefits both to Wal-Mart and its customers.

WAL-MART'S ANSWER TO PARAGRAPH 12

Wal-Mart admits that the referenced meeting took place. As to the "purpose of the meeting" Wal-Mart admits that this most likely was the purpose for which Hood requested the meeting, though the exact intent of Hood for the meeting cannot be admitted or denied by Wal-Mart, it is therefore denied.

AMG'S ALLEGATIONS OF PARAGRAPH 13

In July, 1991, Hood met with Dave Lienemann, the advertising and pricing manager for Hypermart U.S.A., a division or company related to Wal-Mart. The purpose of this meeting was to follow up on the meeting with Glass and to provide more information to Wal-Mart about the Shoppers Calculator. As a result of this meeting, Hood proposed to Lienemann a contractual arrangement

APPENDIX

between AMG and Wal-Mart whereby the Shoppers Calculator would be placed in Hypermart and Wal-Mart Supercenter outlets.

WAL-MART'S ANSWER TO PARAGRAPH 13

As to paragraph 13 of the Complaint, Wal-Mart admits the allegations therein

AMG'S ALLEGATIONS OF PARAGRAPH 14

In September, 1991, AMG and Wal-Mart entered into the first of several related contracts, a copy of which is attached as Exhibit "A". The first contract called for AMG to install Shoppers Calculators in Hypermart and Wal-Mart Supercenters for a period of one year upon completion of a 90-day test program.

WAL-MART'S ANSWER TO PARAGRAPH 14

As to paragraph 14 of the Complaint, Wal-Mart admits the allegations therein with the proviso that Wal-Mart objects to the reference of the contract as being the "first of several related contracts" to the extent that such allegation is intended to imply that the contracts were anything other than separate and distinct contractual relationships. That is, upon the execution of any subsequent contract, that subsequent contract became the sole contractual relationship existing between the parties.

AMG'S ALLEGATIONS OF PARAGRAPH 15

From October, 1991, through March, 1992, AMG conducted research involving the store managers and assistant store managers in the Hypermarts and Supercenters where the Shoppers Calculator had been placed. Virtually all of the store managers and assistant store managers raved about the Shoppers Calculators. No negative comments surfaced in the monthly interviews. During the same time period, Wal-Mart conducted customer interviews to determine the level of customer satisfaction with the Shoppers Calculator. Those interviews established that 63% of all Wal-Mart customers used the Shoppers Calculator, that 75% of those customers used the calculator to track their purchases against their available budgets, and the customers rated the presence of the Shoppers Calculators at 8.5 on a scale of one to ten.

WAL-MART'S ANSWER TO PARAGRAPH 15

232

Wal-Mart admits that an AMG representative conducted surveys or research as indicated, and AMG represented as factual the information contained in this paragraph. Wal-Mart is without first hand knowledge of the allegations and they are therefore deemed denied, with the exception that Wal-Mart generally understands from the survey results that customers did indicate finding the calculators convenient. To the extent additional discovery indicates that any specific allegations should be admitted, Wal-Mart would reserve the right to amend this portion of it's answer.

AMG'S ALLEGATIONS OF PARAGRAPH 16

In April, 1992, AMG presented the results of the management and consumer interviews to Lienemann. The results of these interviews were also submitted to Glass and other Wal-Mart executives, including David Burghart, vice president for store planning. On May 20, 1992, Hood had a meeting with Burghart to discuss the Shoppers Calculator program. In a follow-up letter dated May 21, 1992, Hood reiterated to Burghart that AMG was "confident that such a Shoppers Calculator media vehicle within your stores represents an all new opportunity to tap media funds totally inaccessible to Wal-Mart - or any other retailer - in the past." More specifically, Hood confirmed that the Shoppers Calculator program could be used by Wal-Mart to secure national advertising media funds. Per his conversation with Berghart on May 20, 1992, Hood sent Burghart a new proposed contract to continue the Shoppers Calculator program.

WAL-MART'S ANSWER TO PARAGRAPH 16

To the extent that paragraph 16 represents allegations of actions, letters written or conversations Hood states he had, the allegations are admitted; all other allegations are denied.

AMG'S ALLEGATIONS OF PARAGRAPH 17

In June, 1992, Hood and representatives of Wal-Mart, including Burghart, verbally agreed to the terms of a new contract. By letter dated June 25, 1992, Hood sent to Burghart "clean" copies of the new contract, plus copies showing the changes that had been suggested by Wal-Mart.

WAL-MART'S ANSWER TO PARAGRAPH 17

The allegations are denied with the exception that Wal-Mart admits that the referenced letter of June 25, 1992 was sent by Hood to Wal-Mart.

AMG'S ALLEGATIONS OF PARAGRAPH 18

In July, 1992, Burghart informed Hood that the Shoppers Calculator program had been suspended at the direction of Paul Higham, the vice president of advertising for Wal-Mart Stores. According to Burghart, Higham had suspended the program because he did not want AMG involved in selling in-store advertising for Wal-Mart. Higham was apparently concerned that the program would interfere with Wal-Mart's existing sources for sales promotion revenue. Later in the month, Hood wrote a letter to Bill Fields, the executive vice president for merchandise and sales and explained that the Shoppers Calculator program would not interfere with Wal-Mart's existing sources of revenues from national advertisers. Thereafter, Hood met with Burghart to further explain these matters. Near the end of July, 1992, Hood also visited about these matters with Paul Higham in Wal-Mart's marketing department.

WAL-MART'S ANSWER TO PARAGRAPH 18

As to paragraph 18 of the Complaint, Wal-Mart admits the allegations therein.

AMG'S ALLEGATIONS OF PARAGRAPH 19

As a consequence of these discussions, Wal-Mart decided to go forward with the Shoppers Calculator program with a change in the advertising sales responsibility. A revised version of the contract was prepared whereby the Shoppers Calculator would be installed in the Bentonville Supercenter for a 90-day test period that would be visible to Wal-Mart's senior management, whose offices are located in Bentonville. During this test period, Wal-Mart was to conduct additional customer interviews and advertise private label products to determine the impact of the Shoppers Calculator program on Wal-Mart and its customers.

WAL-MART'S ANSWER TO PARAGRAPH 19

As to paragraph 19 of the Complaint, Wal-Mart denies all allegations with the exception that Wal-Mart admits that after further discussion and consideration it did decide to allow a very limited 90-day test period relating to the Bentonville, Super Center.

AMG'S ALLEGATIONS OF PARAGRAPH 20

On or about August 24, 1992, AMG installed the Shoppers Calculator in the Bentonville Supercenter. At approximately the same time, Wal-Mart provided AMG with store traffic counts and marketing data for use by AMG in making presentations to national advertisers. By this time, Loveless had become the key contact person for AMG.

WAL-MART'S ANSWER TO PARAGRAPH 20

As to paragraph 20 of the Complaint, Wal-Mart admits the allegations therein

AMG'S ALLEGATIONS OF PARAGRAPH 21

The Shoppers Calculator was enthusiastically received by the Bentonville Supercenter store manager. In late August and early September, 1992, a Wal-Mart store manager from Mississippi contacted AMG to find out how he could get the Shoppers Calculator placed in his store.

WAL-MART'S ANSWER TO PARAGRAPH 21

As to paragraph 21 of the Complaint, Wal-Mart admits the allegations with the proviso that the plaintiff's use of the word "enthusiastically" simply indicated that the manager saw the calculator as a convenience to the customer. If anything further is meant by the allegation, then it is therefore denied. The remaining portions of paragraph 21 are denied.

AMG'S ALLEGATIONS OF PARAGRAPH 22

On September 24, 1992, Hood wrote to Loveless requesting answers to questions that had been posed to Loveless in July and August. This information was required in order for AMG to sell the program on the national advertising budgets of Wal-Mart's vendors.

WAL-MART'S ANSWER TO PARAGRAPH 22

Wal-Mart admits Hood wrote a letter of September 24, 1992, to Loveless and as the remaining allegations are incomplete and may be misinterpreted, they are denied.

AMG'S ALLEGATIONS OF PARAGRAPH 23

From September through December, 1992, AMG conducted a concentrated sales calling program on the national advertising accounts of Wal-Mart's vendors. The response of the vendors was overwhelmingly positive. During this time period, AMG presented numerous advertising insert approaches to Loveless for use in the test program at the Bentonville Supercenter. Loveless rejected all of the proposals, leading AMG to believe that Wal-Mart did not need to verify AMG's sales data.

WAL-MART'S ANSWER TO PARAGRAPH 23

As to the allegations as to actions or conduct of AMG, Wal-Mart admits that the AMG representative that took those actions and received those responses, Wal-Mart is without independent verification of same and they are therefore denied. As to actions by Wal-Mart the allegations are denied.

AMG'S ALLEGATIONS OF PARAGRAPH 24

The 90-day test period at the Bentonville Supercenter was completed in early December, 1992. Immediately thereafter, Hood contacted Loveless to set up a meeting with Wal-Mart to discuss the program. During this conversation, Loveless told Hood that Wal-Mart had validated AMG's sales data and that Wal-Mart's executive management was very pleased with the results of the test program. Loveless further told Hood that Wal-Mart's senior management executives were too busy to meet with AMG until after the holidays. A meeting was scheduled on January 5, 1993. Prior to the meeting, Hood provided Wal-Mart with additional information about the results of the test program.

WAL-MART'S ANSWER TO PARAGRAPH 24

Wal-Mart admits the allegations of paragraph 24, with the proviso that Wal-Mart denies that any representative stated that Wal-Mart had validated AMG's sale data.

AMG'S ALLEGATIONS OF PARAGRAPH 25

In the morning of January 5, 1993, Loveless called Hood to cancel the meeting because certain senior management executives were unavailable. During this conversation, Loveless told Hood that Wal-Mart was very plead with the program and that Fields had made a decision to have the Shoppers Calculators installed in more than 500 stores. Loveless told Hood that, as a result of internal meetings held earlier in the day, the only question remaining was whether Wal-Mart or AMG would sell the advertising. Based on these and other verbal commitments from Wal-Mart representatives, Hood and Young personally guaranteed an additional $100,000 of corporate bank loans. AMG's directors also guaranteed an additional $50,000 of bank loans in reliance on Wal-Mart's representations regarding the future of the Shoppers Calculator program.

WAL-MART'S ANSWER TO PARAGRAPH 25

Wal-Mart admits that the phone call was held approximately January 5, 1993, and that Loveless would have indicated general positive reaction to the program. However, all other allegations are denied and specifically Wal-Mar is without any information or knowledge as to what actions AMG took following the phone call, and they are specifically denied. Further, it is specifically denied that any "commitment" was made by Loveless or any other representative on January 5, 1993.

AMG'S ALLEGATIONS OF PARAGRAPH 26

On January 8, 1993, Hood wrote a letter to Loveless providing additional information about the program and making suggestions about how to allocate the costs associated with selling advertising. Another meeting was scheduled for February 4, 1993, and Hood emphasized the importance of Wal-Mart providing certain information at that meeting so that the program could move forward.

WAL-MART'S ANSWER TO PARAGRAPH 26

The allegations of paragraph 26, are admitted to the extent that Hood wrote a letter January 28, 1993, and another meeting was scheduled February 4, 1993; the balance of the allegations are denied.

AMG'S ALLEGATIONS OF PARAGRAPH 27

Only Loveless and Barbara Brown showed up at the meeting on February 4, 1993. (Brown also worked in Wal-Mart's marketing department.) During this meeting, Loveless and Brown told Hood and Cindy Hood (director of sales for AMG) that Wal-Mart was still working on getting the information that had been requested by Hood. They said that Wal-Mart should be ready to move forward within two weeks. Hood discussed with Loveless and Brown the terms of a new contract. Hood confirmed some of these discussions in a letter to Brown dated February 5, 1993.

WAL-MART'S ANSWER TO PARAGRAPH 27

APPENDIX

The general allegations of paragraph 27 are admitted with the proviso that representations made by Wal-Mart representatives with regards to "ready to move forward within two weeks" indicated a statement of its intent of the likelihood of entering into a contractual agreement, sometime possibly in the future. Wal-Mart admits that Hood wrote a letter dated February 15, 1993, but denies that the letter accurately reports portions of the discussion.

AMG'S ALLEGATIONS OF PARAGRAPH 28

In a letter to Fields dated February 9, 1993, Hood thanked Fields for Wal-Mart's decision to allow AMG to begin installing the Shoppers Calculator in more Wal-Mart stores. In a letter to Loveless of the same date, Hood thanked Loveless for calling on February 8th and confirmed that Loveless would be calling back later in the week with the needed information that had not yet been provided.

WAL-MART'S ANSWER TO PARAGRAPH 28

Wal-Mart admits AMG's allegations that it wrote two letters on February 9, 1993, but Wal-Mart does not admit the accuracy of the content of either letter.

AMG'S ALLEGATIONS OF PARAGRAPH 29

On February 11, 1993, much to Hood's surprise, Loveless telephone (sic) Hood to tell him the results of a meeting involving Higham. According to Loveless, Higham said that "he did not want AMG involved in any of the Wal-Mart advertising, and therefore, did not want to roll out the Shoppers Calculator's service."

WAL-MART'S ANSWER TO PARAGRAPH 29

Not having recorded the conversation, Wal-Mart is not able to admit or deny the specific words quoted by plaintiff in the Complaint; However, Wal-Mart generally agrees that the information conveyed by Loveless on February 11, 1993 was to the effect stated by plaintiff's.

AMG'S ALLEGATIONS OF PARAGRAPH 30

On February 12, 1993, Hood wrote a letter to Higham expressing surprise about his decision in light of the test results and the representations that had been made by various representatives of

238

Walmart's EGONOMICS

Wal-Mart about Wal-Mart's intention to go forward with the program. Hood requested a meeting with Higham to discuss the status of the program.

WAL-MART'S ANSWER TO PARAGRAPH 30

Again, Wal-Mart admits that Hood wrote the letter referenced to February 12, 1993, but does not admit the accuracy of the contents of such letter.

AMG'S ALLEGATIONS OF PARAGRAPH 31

On February 15, 1993, Hood contacted Higham by telephone. During this conversation, Higham agreed to meet with Hood on February 24, 1993. On February 16, 1993, Hood wrote a letter to Higham confirming the meeting and providing additional information about the program. In this letter, Hood confirmed that Higham's position regarding AMG selling advertising was "totally contrary to the testing direction given to us last August."

WAL-MART'S ANSWER TO PARAGRAPH 31

Wal-Mart admits the allegations with regards to the phone call that limited allegations with regards to the February 15, 1993 phone call; Wal-Mart further admits that Hood wrote a letter on February 16, 1993. Wal-Mart does not admit the accuracy, contention or allegation made by AMG in the referenced letter. Specifically, in while AMG may not have intended this interpretation, Wal-Mart interprets the last sentence of the paragraph to indicate that Higham acknowledged to AMG that Wal-Mart's position was totally contrary to testing direction. If this is the intent of the allegation, it is specifically denied.

AMG'S ALLEGATIONS OF PARAGRAPH 32

On February 24, 1993, Hood met with Higham and Brown. Also present at the meeting was Gary Young, the executive vice president of AMG. During this meeting, Higham expressed an interest in continuing the program and selling AMG's "packaged goods" calculator concept to vendors. The use of "credit card calculators" was especially appealing to Higham. At the close of the meeting, Higham promised to reconsider his decision and "get back with" AMG.

WAL-MART'S ANSWER TO PARAGRAPH 32

As to paragraph 32 of the Complaint, Wal-Mart admits the allegations therein.

239

AMG'S ALLEGATIONS OF PARAGRAPH 33

On February 25, 1993, Hood wrote a letter to Higham enclosing a recap of all the research on the use of the Shoppers Calculator in Wal-Mart stores. Hood further said that he would contact Higham on March 3, 1993, for the purpose of continuing their discussions. After several unsuccessful efforts to reach Higham by telephone, and after several telephone calls were not returned, Hood was able to reach Higham by telephone on March 8, 1993. In this conversation Higham told Hood that Wal-Mart's buyers were "unwilling to mess with the calculators," but that Visa and Discovery cards might be interested in the program. Hood asked Higham whether Wal-Mart had done anything to determine the calculator's impact on Wal-Mart's sales. Higham responded by saying it would be impossible to make such a determination. The same day, Hood wrote another letter to Higham enclosing sketches that might be helpful in soliciting the Visa and Discovery card accounts.

WAL-MART'S ANSWER TO PARAGRAPH 33

Allegations of paragraph 33 are admitted, with the exception that Higham denies failing to return telephone calls and further cannot admit the language appearing in quotations as Higham did not have the conversation recorded. Nevertheless, Wal-Mart would admit that Higiiman would have indicated to Hood that the Wal-Mart buyers were concerned that the Shopper's Calculator program did not provide the proper value to Wal-Mart and/or the vendors involved.

AMG'S ALLEGATIONS OF PARAGRAPH 34

On March 31, 1993, Hood wrote another letter to Higham in which he outlined Wal-Mart's failure to get back in touch with AMG and Wal-Mart's contradictory instructions and statements regarding the program. In this letter, Hood requested an immediate commitment from Wal-Mart about the future of the program. Higham responded to this letter by letter dated April 6, 1993. Higham told Hood that he was "still working with the potential resources." Higham also said "I know it must be frustrating waiting. Please be patient."

WAL-MART'S ANSWER TO PARAGRAPH 34

As to paragraph 34 of the Complaint, Wal-Mart admits the allegations therein with the proviso that the comments attributed to Higham were made from the standpoint of Hood's acknowledgment. Wal-Mart was free to make the decision it wanted to with regards to the Shopper's Calculator program, and Highams acknowledgment that he understood that it would reasonably be frustrating for one such as Hood to wait while Wal-Mart considered various business options before making the final business decision. If this is the intent of the allegation by plaintiff, then the allegation is admitted. If some other intent was intended by the allegation, this is denied. Wal-Mart does not admit that the content of the letter referenced by plaintiff.

AMG'S ALLEGATIONS OF PARAGRAPH 35

On April 28, 1993, Higham wrote to Hood stating Wal-Mart's intention to place the Shoppers Calculator in "an additional 200 stores for continuation of our on-going test." In this letter, Higham said that the "sole factor for final approval will be the judgment of our buyers as to whether or not the cost of advertising on the calculators will have any deleterious effect on our cost of goods." Higham said that Loveless would be the "primary contact" with AMG and that Brown would be the "executive sponsor."

WAL-MART'S ANSWER TO PARAGRAPH 35

As to paragraph 35 of the Complaint, Wal-Mart admits the allegations therein

AMG'S ALLEGATIONS OF PARAGRAPH 36

By letter dated May 5, 1993, Hood enclosed an updated version of the contract that was originally agreed upon in June, 1992, with the changes necessary to make the contract current.

WAL-MART'S ANSWER TO PARAGRAPH 36

Wal-Mart admits that Hood wrote the letter dated May 5, 1993 and provided with it a version of a contract, but Wal-Mart specifically denies the allegations of this paragraph to the extent that they imply that any such contractual terms were agreed to in June of 1992, or at any other time.

AMG'S ALLEGATIONS OF PARAGRAPH 37

241

APPENDIX

On May 5, 1993, Loveless called Hood and told him that Wal-Mart had already begun selling advertising for the Shoppers Calculator program and needed the contract with AMG to be signed as soon as possible.

WAL-MART'S ANSWER TO PARAGRAPH 37

As to paragraph 37 of the Complaint, Wal-Mart denies the allegation therein, other than the list did not indicate the contract with AMG needed to be finalized.

AMG'S ALLEGATIONS OF PARAGRAPH 38

On June 8, 1993, Loveless contacted Hood by telephone and told him that of all the advertisers contacted by Wal-Mart, only one had declined, and the response from the others was quite positive.

WAL-MART'S ANSWER TO PARAGRAPH 38

As to paragraph 38 of the Complaint, Wal-Mart denies the allegation therein. In fact the representations were made by Hood to Loveless rather than Loveless to Hood.

AMG'S ALLEGATIONS OF PARAGRAPH 39

After further discussions between Hood and Loveless regarding the status of the contract, the second in the series of contracts between AMG and Wal-Mart was executed on or about June 28, 1993. A copy of this contract is attached Exhibit "B".

WAL-MART'S ANSWER TO PARAGRAPH 39

Admitted to the extent that the paragraph indicates a new and separate contract was executed on or about June 28, 1993. While it is unclear what plaintiff meant by it's reference "in the series of contracts by AMG and Wal-Mart", Wal-Mart would specifically deny that any previous contractual relationship survived the execution of the June 28, 1993 contract. This latter contract was the sole contractual obligation in rights existing between the parties.

AMG'S ALLEGATIONS OF PARAGRAPH 40

On July 29, 1993, Loveless provided AMG with an internal Wal-Mart memo authored by Loveless regarding the Shoppers Calculator program, which memo had been copied to Higham and Brown. Among other things, the memo said "vendors are to utilize sampling dollars (no national advertising dollars)." Hood contacted Loveless the same day to tell him that this statement in the

242

memo was contrary to the statements made by other Wal-Mart representatives, including Higham, in that vendors were to utilize national advertising dollars - not sampling or promotional dollars to which Wal-Mart already had access.

WAL-MART'S ANSWER TO PARAGRAPH 40

As to paragraph 40 of the Complaint, Wal-Mart admits the allegations therein.

AMG'S ALLEGATIONS OF PARAGRAPH 41

Thereafter, after several unsuccessful attempts, Hood reached Higham by telephone on August 25, 1993, and advised Higham that the memo was in error. Hood also advised Higham that national advertisers were continuing to call AMG for program details and that, two months after the contract had been signed, it appeared that Wal-Mart had not contacted any of the national advertisers. Higham responded by telling Hood that Loveless was running the program and that Higham did not have time to supervise him. Hood wrote a letter to Higham the same day confirming that numerous national advertisers had contacted AMG and had stated their desire to advertise in Wal-Mart stores using the Shoppers Calculator.

WAL-MART'S ANSWER TO PARAGRAPH 41

With reference to "unsuccessful attempts", the allegation is denied. Wal-Mart further denies that when plaintiff stated he did not have to supervise Loveless; whereas the general observation made was that Loveless was the person responsible to implement the program and that he could not oversee every aspect of Lovelessness' efforts. Though Wal-Mart disagrees with the content of the communication in the letter, Wal-Mart admits the balance of the allegations with regards to allegations made by Hood and the fact that he authored the letter referenced.

AMG'S ALLEGATIONS OF PARAGRAPH 42

On September 10, 1993, Cindy Hood of AMG spoke with Loveless and was informed that Wal-Mart's buyers had asked for additional time to negotiate the Shoppers Calculator advertising contracts. Loveless told Cindy Hood that he was sending a memo to all Wal-Mart buyers extending their deadline to September 22, 1993. During the next week, Cindy Hood unsuccessfully attempted to reach Loveless by telephone several times to get an update on the status of the Shoppers Calculator

APPENDIX

program. Cindy Hood eventually reached Loveless on September 21, 1993. Loveless told Cindy Hood that he would check on the status of the program and call her back later in the day. Loveless did not call back. On September 22, 1993, Cindy Hood telephoned Loveless again regarding the status of the contact with national advertisers. Loveless said that he would provide this information to AMG in a few days. When Cindy Hood requested the list of 200 additional stores for planning purposes, Loveless told Cindy Hood that "his hands were tied" and that AMG could not get the list until the ads were sold.

WAL-MART'S ANSWER TO PARAGRAPH 42

All allegations are admitted with the exception that plaintiff attempts to imply that Loveless does not return phone calls in a timely manner, which is contrary to his routine business practice. Further, it was made clear that the list of the two hundred additional stores was something being considered by Wal-Mart. Further, Loveless denies making a comment to the effect "his hands were tied". Though he would have indicated he was currently unable to provide the list of proposed stores until he had been able to work out the details with all of the operations personnel. Wal-Mart further denies stating that the store would not be provided until the advertisements were sold, in fact it was recognized that the ability to sell advertisements was not dependent upon finalizing the proposed store list.

AMG'S ALLEGATIONS OF PARAGRAPH 43

On September 30, 1993, Hood wrote another letter to Glass stating that Wal-Mart had not made any efforts to sell the program, much less the "best efforts" that were required by the contract.

WAL-MART'S ANSWER TO PARAGRAPH 43

Wal-Mart admits the referenced letter was written, but does not admit the contents of the letter.

AMG'S ALLEGATIONS OF PARAGRAPH 44

On December 8, 1993, after more than 20 unsuccessful efforts to reach Loveless by telephone, Cindy Hood made contact with Loveless by phone and asked him about the status of the program. Loveless acted very surprised that AMG had not previously been contacted by Higham. Loveless was

244

under the impression that Higham had contacted AMG several months earlier to inform AMG of Wal-Mart's decision not to go forward with the Shoppers Calculator program. Loveless told Cindy Hood again that "his hands were tied." He said, however, that he would contact Higham and get back in touch with Cindy Hood. Loveless never called back.

WAL-MART'S ANSWER TO PARAGRAPH 44

Allegations are admitted with the exception that again Loveless denies that there would have been 20 phone calls made without his returning such calls, which would be contrary to his business and that of other persons. Further, Wal-Mart would deny Loveless made any statement to the effect "his hands were tied" and did understand that Paul Higham would be contacted and get back to Cindy Hood.

AMG'S ALLEGATIONS OF PARAGRAPH 45

On December 8, 1993, Hood wrote to Glass and asked Glass to have someone contact AMG immediately regarding the status of the program. Hood once again told Glass that Wal-Mart had not contacted any advertisers in an effort to sell the program. Hood further explained that AMG was continuing to spend tens of thousands of dollars each month maintaining the program in the original test stores, that AMG had spent hundreds of thousands of dollars on research, installation, and maintenance, and that Wal-Mart's failure to perform its obligations under the contract was causing a delay in a $2 million private placement for capital by AMG.

WAL-MART'S ANSWER TO PARAGRAPH 45

Wal-Mart admits the allegation to the extent it states that plaintiff authored the letter of December 8, 1993, but does not admit the contents of the letter.

AMG'S ALLEGATIONS OF PARAGRAPH 46

On December 9, 1993, Higham wrote to Hood and acknowledged that he had met with Glass to discuss Hood's letter of December 8, 1993. Higham said that "we continue to believe that our decision not to participate is in our best interest." Higham said that Loveless would work with AMG in the process of removing the calculators from the Wal-Mart stores.

WAL-MART'S ANSWER TO PARAGRAPH 46

As to paragraph 46 of the Complaint, Wal-Mart admits the allegations therein.

AMG'S ALLEGATIONS OF PARAGRAPH 47

On December 14, 1993, Hood wrote a letter to Higham alleging that Wal-Mart had purposely mislead AMG and had breached its contractual obligation to use best efforts to sell the program. Higham responded to Hood in a letter dated December 28, 1993, stating that Wal-Mart had acted in accordance with its contractual obligations and in good faith.

WAL-MART'S ANSWER TO PARAGRAPH 47

As to paragraph 2 of the Complaint, Wal-Mart admits the allegations therein to the extent that Wal-Mart acknowledges the two referenced letters were written, but does not admit the contents of the letter of December 14, 1993 by plaintiff.

AMG'S ALLEGATIONS OF PARAGRAPH 48

In early January, 1994, AMG's counsel, Gable & Gotwals of Tulsa, contacted Wal-Mart and threatened legal action if Wal-Mart was not willing to promptly meet and reconsider its position,. as outlined in Higham's letter of December 28, 1993. Thereafter, a meeting was held with members of Wal-Mart's legal department. As a result of these discussions, Wal-Mart reversed its position and stated its intent to proceed with the Shoppers Calculator program. Discussions, negotiations, and correspondence regarding a new contractual arrangement occurred throughout the first half of 1994.

WAL-MART'S ANSWER TO PARAGRAPH 48

As to paragraph 48 of the Complaint, Wal-Mart admits the allegations therein with the exception that Wal-Mart would take issue with plaintiff's characterization that Wal-Mart "reversed it's position" as what occurred was good faith, bona fide discussions between the parties, which allowed for his concerns and issues to be dealt with in the context of a proposed new contractual arrangement.

AMG'S ALLEGATIONS OF PARAGRAPH 49

On or about June 24, 1994, AMG and Wal-Mart entered into the third in the series of contracts regarding the Shoppers Calculator program. A copy of this contract is attached as Exhibit "C". Among other things, this contract contained a provision obligating Wal-Mart to support all advertising sales efforts by providing information to AMG and/or potential advertisers. Under the terms of this contract, the Shoppers Calculator was to be installed and maintained in the Bentonville Supercenter and all of Wal-Mart's stores located in Regions 2 and 9 (comprising over 220 stores in Texas, Arkansas, and Oklahoma).

WAL-MART'S ANSWER TO PARAGRAPH 49

As to paragraph 49 of the Complaint, Wal-Mart admits the allegations therein with the exception again of not admitting to the characterization of the June 24, 1994, contract as "third in the series" regarding the Shoppers Calculator program, if the intention of plaintiff at making the allegation was to indicate to the court that the preceding contracts were still in effect or were to be considered by the court. The June 24, 1994, contract completely replaced and represented an entirely new and sole contractual relationship between the parties.

AMG'S ALLEGATIONS OF PARAGRAPH 50

On September 28, 1994, by mutual agreement, AMG and Wal-Mart entered into a first amendment to the third contract that was executed in June, 1994. The purpose of the amendment was to extend the term of the contract from 12 months to 18 months.

WAL-MART'S ANSWER TO PARAGRAPH 50

As to paragraph 50 of the Complaint, Wal-Mart admits the allegations therein with the proviso that Wal-Mart objects to the reference of the June contract being "the third contract", if plaintiff seeks to imply that the preceding contracts continued to have any force and effect between the parties. Otherwise, the allegation is admitted.

AMG'S ALLEGATIONS OF PARAGRAPH 51

Beginning in the Fall of 1994, AMG learned from various third parties that Wal-Mart buyers were actively and specifically discouraging vendors from participating in the Shoppers Calculator program. For example, a representative of Russell Corporation stated that a Wal-Mart buyer had said that Wal-Mart preferred that Russell Corporation participate in other Wal-Mart programs, not the Shoppers Calculator program. The director of promotions for Heinz expressed a lack of interest in the Shoppers Calculator program because Wal-Mart buyers had asked Heinz not to participate in "these types of programs." A representative of Procter & Gamble Co. similarly stated that AMG

APPENDIX

could not become a core supplier for Procter & Gamble's in-store advertising program with Wal-Mart. (AMG had previously been on Procter & Gamble's core supplier list.) AMG sales representative Gene Bay contacted Hood on November 1, 1994, and related his feeling that Wal-Mart was deliberately sabotaging the Shoppers Calculator program. The same day, Cadbury Beverages contacted AMG and related that a Wal-Mart buyer had specifically told Cadbury not to participate in the program. The buyer refused to give Cadbury a specific reason why Wal-Mart did not want Cadbury to participate. A representative of Pepsi Cola was told by a Wal-Mart buyer that the Shoppers Calculator program did not work and that Wal-Mart did not want Pepsi Cola to participate in the program. A representative of Block Drug Company was told by a Wal-Mart buyer that Block Drug Company would be much better off running special programs with Wal-Mart instead of participating in the Shoppers Calculator program. On or about November 1, 1994, after discovering the extend and consequences of Wal-Mart's negative statements to potential advertisers regarding the Shoppers Calculator program, AMG was forced to cancel another private offering to sell common stock.

WAL-MART'S ANSWER TO PARAGRAPH 51

Wal-Mart has no information as to the accuracy or inaccuracy as to the allegation, but admits that the general information contained has been represented by plaintiffs to be factual. Not having adequate information to know the accuracy of the statement, they are denied. Specifically, Wal-Mart denies having any knowledge as to what decisions AMG made or did not make with regards to a private offering and has no knowledge as to any issues that may have impacted that decision.

AMG'S ALLEGATIONS OF PARAGRAPH 52

After hearing and documenting such conversations, AMG contacted Wal-Mart and expressed concern with the information that was being provided to vendors by Wal-Mart buyers. AMG requested assistance from Wal-Mart to make clear to potential advertisers that Wal-Mart had not "written off" the Shoppers Calculator program. Wal-Mart refused to provide any such information to potential advertisers, further evidencing Wal-Mart's bad faith plan to sabotage the program. As a consequence of Wal-Mart's bad faith efforts and false statements to advertisers, AMG's ability to

248

market the Shoppers Calculator through Wal-Mart and other retail chains has been seriously jeopardized.

WAL-MART'S ANSWER TO PARAGRAPH 52

Wal-Mart does not know to what extent plaintiff has heard or documented any conversations with vendors or others, and therefore, the allegation is denied. Wal-Mart admits that AMG contacted Wal-Mart and expressed concern about the information being provided to vendors by Wal-Mart buyers and that AMG did request certain clarification from Wal-Mart, in this regard AMG provided to Wal-Mart a proposed memo to buyers and potential advertisers, the content of which was found objectionable in part by Wal-Mart. Wal-Mart proposed an alternative form of memorandum and submitted it to AMG for its consideration, and requested an opportunity to meet further on the matter. Rather than responding to Wal-Mart's proposed modifications, AMG not only did not respond, but did not have any further communication with Wal-Mart on the subject. Wal-Mart is specifically unable to respond to AMG's allegations with regards to the impact of any actions it took on AMG's ability to market it's product to other retail chains, and the allegation thereof is denied.

AMG'S ALLEGATIONS OF PARAGRAPH 53

Wal-Mart made false representations of material fact to AMG.

WAL-MART'S ANSWER TO PARAGRAPH 53

As to paragraph 53 of the Complaint, Wal-Mart denies the allegation therein.

AMG'S ALLEGATIONS OF PARAGRAPH 54

Wal-Mart knew or believed that such representations were false or did not have a sufficient basis of information to make such representations.

WAL-MART'S ANSWER TO PARAGRAPH 54

As to paragraph 54 of the Complaint, Wal-Mart denies the allegation therein.

AMG'S ALLEGATIONS OF PARAGRAPH 55

Wal-Mart made such false representations for the purpose of inducing AMG to forego legal action, to continue to spend and raise substantial sums of money on the Shoppers Calculator program, and to induce AMG to enter into another written contract, all to the benefit of Wal-Mart and the detriment of AMG.

WAL-MART'S ANSWER TO PARAGRAPH 55

As to paragraph 55 of the Complaint, Wal-Mart denies the allegation therein.

AMG'S ALLEGATIONS OF PARAGRAPH 56

AMG justifiably relied upon the representations of Wal-Mart in deciding to forego legal action, in deciding to spend and raise substantial sums of money on the Shoppers Calculator program, and in deciding to enter into written contracts with Wal-Mart. As a consequence, AMG suffered damages in an amount to be determined at trial.

WAL-MART'S ANSWER TO PARAGRAPH 56

As to paragraph 4 of the Complaint, Wal-Mart denies the allegation therein.

AMG'S ALLEGATIONS OF PARAGRAPH 57

AMG and Wal-Mart had a contractual relationship, as evidenced by the series of related contracts between the parties, all of which should be considered as a matter of law to be a single, integrated contract.

WAL-MART'S ANSWER TO PARAGRAPH 57

As to paragraph 57 of the Complaint, Wal-Mart denies the allegation therein. As of the time of filing this lawsuit, the parties have a single contractual relationship existing between them which is the contract of June, 1994.

AMG'S ALLEGATIONS OF PARAGRAPH 58

Wal-Mart breached its obligations under the contracts by violating both the written terms of the contracts and the implied obligation to deal with AMG in good faith.

WAL-MART'S ANSWER TO PARAGRAPH 58

As to paragraph 4 of the Complaint, Wal-Mart denies the allegation therein.

AMG'S ALLEGATIONS OF PARAGRAPH 59

At the time of contracting with AMG, Wal-Mart knew that a breach of the contractual agreement by Wal-Mart would result in substantial consequential damages to AMG and its

The intentional/negligent disruption of such contractual relationships and business expectancies of AMG was a proximate cause of damages that have been suffered by AMG, in an amount to be determined at trial.

WAL-MART'S ANSWER TO PARAGRAPH 64

As to paragraph 64 of the Complaint, Wal-Mart denies the allegation therein.

ADDITIONAL ANSWERS AND AFFIRMATIVE DEFENSES

65.   At all times Wal-Mart has acted in a good faith performance of its contractual obligation with the plaintiff pursuant to the terms of that contract of June, 1994.

66.   Wal-Mart has not breached it's contract with plaintiff and continues to advise plaintiff of its willingness to proceed forward with the contract, though plaintiff indicates an unwillingness or inability to perform its obligations under the contract.

67.   Affirmative defense of assumption of risk.

68.   Affirmative defense of contributory negligence.

69.   Affirmative defense of estoppel.

70.   Affirmative defense of waiver.

71.   Affirmative defense of waiver.

72.   Plaintiff has failed to mitigate damages and thus is precluded from any recovery against the defendant.

73.   In the event plaintiff continues in its failure to comply with its contractual obligations, Wal-Mart is entitled to a declaration from this court that is relieved from any obligations under the contract.

74.   Wal-Mart reserves the right, as discovery is ongoing to amend this answer to include any additional defenses and/or to assert a counter claim against plaintiff for any other responsible party.

Respectfully Submitted,

Wal-Mart Stores, Inc.

By: _____
Jon B. Comstock, OBA #1836
Corporate Litigation Counsel
Wal-Mart Stores, Inc.
702 S.W. 8th Street
Bentonville, Arkansas 72716
(501) 273-4505
(501) 273-8650 (Fax)

Attorneys for Defendant
Wal-Mart Stores, Inc.

CERTIFICATE OF MAILING

I hereby certify that on the 22 day of February, 1995, a true and exact copy of the above and foregoing document was mailed, by U.S. Mail with postage thereon fully prepaid, to:

Thomas A. Mars, Esq.
EVERETT, MARS & STILLS
P. O. Box 1646
Fayetteville, AR 72702-1646

By: _____
Jon B. Comstock

BACKGROUND OF CHARLES H. "CHUCK" HOOD

Hood is a veteran of more than forty years in the advertising, marketing and public relations businesses. From 1969 until 1990, Hood served as co-founder and chairman of Hood, Hope and Associates. He later served as chairman of Ackerman, Hood and McQueen. At the time of his retirement from the advertising agency business, the agency was ranked as the 108th largest advertising agency in America, having offices in six cities, 200 employees, and billings in excess of $80 million annually.

After departing from the advertising agency business, Hood purchased a patent for "calculators on shopping carts." He then further-developed and improved the concept to include an advertising-image area, and founded the ADDvantage Media Group, Inc. — an in-store advertising company having its "Shopper's Calculators" on carts in a network of grocery and mass merchant chains. He later took the company public and served as its president and CEO for ten years, prior to the company being forced to close its doors and sell its public shell in September, 1999.

Hood is a past member of the "*Advertising Age*" Editorial Review Board, the board of the American Association of Advertising Agencies (AAAA), and the board of POPAI (Point of Purchase Advertising Institute). He has filled numerous regional and national positions within each. Hood is a past recipient of the Tulsa Advertising Federation's Silver Addy (Ad Man of the Year) award, and many other national, regional and local awards. Hood is on the Advisory Board of the University of Tulsa, School of Journalism. He is a graduate of the University of Missouri's School of Journalism, where he received a degree in advertising.

Currently he is a marketing and public relations consultant to several public and privately-held companies. Hood and his wife have four children and seven grandchildren, and reside in Tulsa, OK.

www.ingramcontent.com/pod-product-compliance
Lightning Source LLC
Chambersburg PA
CBHW071408170526
45165CB00001B/216